Caterpillar Soup at 30,000 Feet

Caterpillar Soup at 30,000 Feet
The Leader's Guide to Mastering Your Greatest Transformation

Ben Morley

©2026 All Rights Reserved. No portion of this book may be reproduced, stored in a retrieval system, or transmitted in any form or by any means—electronic, mechanical, photocopy, recording, scanning, or other—except for brief quotations in critical reviews or articles without the prior permission of the author.

Published by Game Changer Publishing

Paperback ISBN: 979-8-90158-207-7
Hardcover ISBN: 979-8-90158-139-1
Digital ISBN: 979-8-90158-141-4

www.GameChangerPublishing.com

DEDICATION

For Fevilyn, Trinity, Natasha, and Samantha—

God gave me the message. He gave me you to carry it home to.

Through every season of becoming—the disorienting, the difficult, and the beautiful—you were my constant. This book is for the world, but you are why it was written.

I love you beyond words. These will have to do.

ADVANCE PRAISE

A hope-filled invitation to pause, reflect, and emerge renewed. With honest storytelling and well-timed reflection, Ben guides leaders to rediscover who they are beneath the noise. It's insightful, practical, and deeply renewing—a resource I'm genuinely excited to recommend.

—Tori Dabasinskas, LMFT, LPCC | Founder, Mirador Retreats

Drawing upon his extensive experience as a military officer and business consultant, Ben Morley has written an honest and insightful book that promotes authentic personal and professional transformation. Moreover, he provides readers with thoughtful, detailed action plans to succeed on the often challenging journey toward realizing their full potential to create value and provide meaningful service to others. Highly recommended.

—Jeffrey J. Matthews, PhD, MBA | George F. Jewett Distinguished Professor Emeritus | University Of Puget Sound | School of Business & Leadership

There is something incredibly grounding about learning leadership from someone who had to make life-altering decisions at 30,000 feet. Ben Morley seamlessly weaves together the precision of a C-17 pilot with a deeply human approach to identity and service. The direction, guidance, and execution plan outlined in this book are worth celebrating. You cannot work through this book and be the same person on the other side. This not only challenges you to adjust your perspectives but also provides practical steps and insights to guide your journey. The roadmap style of this book lays out the flight plan you need. This book parallels leadership principles and guided reflections for your own personal growth.

—Nate Green, Award-Winning CEO | Keynote Speaker | Bestselling Author | Entrepreneur | Success & Performance Coach

Every barrier I broke required me to become someone I hadn't been before. That process is uncomfortable, disorienting, and necessary. Ben Morley explains that process clearly in *Caterpillar Soup at 30,000 Feet.* Any leader navigating change can benefit from this book.

—Samantha Domingue, U.S. Army Major, First Cavalry-Qualified Female to Command a Troop in the U.S. Army | First Female Washington National Guard Ranger School Graduate

Ten years in the US Army as an Army Officer and Platoon Leader has taught me that the leaders who survive uncertainty are the ones who have done the hard work of knowing who they are before the pressure hits. Ben Morley captures that truth with remarkable clarity in *Caterpillar Soup at 30,000 Feet.* This is essential reading for any leader navigating significant change—in the boardroom or in more serious situations with lives on the line.

—Amani Harris, First Vice President, Portfolio Manager, Top Wealth Management Firm | U.S. Army Veteran and Former U.S. Army Officer

Through his remarkably skillful use of leadership lessons learned—hard-earned through personal endeavor and professional experience as both a military aviator and business consultant—Morley's deft ability to make sense of the essential connection between the totally transformed old self and the emergence of a new, more capable leader is profound. By reframing transformation not as a gentle and predictable change but as total dissolution and radical redefinition, this book provides an essential roadmap for anyone navigating their own personal and professional growth into a renowned leader.

—William J. Bender, USAF Lt Gen (Ret) | Five-time Operational Commander | Former U.S. Air Force Chief Information Officer | Industry Executive | Corporate Board Director and Strategic Advisor

In the cockpit, the leaders who fail are the ones who mistake the role for the person. Ben Morley goes straight to the root—who you are when the title is gone. This book is essential. Read it before you need it.

—Lt Col (ret.) Jason O. Harris, USAF Academy Graduate, Combat Veteran | Founder of No Fail Trust

I've spent my life navigating transformation—from the military to multiple leadership roles across technology, startups, global business, and eventually private wealth. What I've learned is that real change is never clean or linear—it's uncomfortable, disorienting, and deeply personal.

This book captures that reality with rare clarity. The concept of the "cocoon" isn't just a metaphor—it's the lived experience of anyone who has had to let go of a former identity to step into something new. It's about the courage to let go of who you've been in order to become who you're capable of being.

For leaders navigating transition, uncertainty, or growth, this book provides both a framework and the reassurance that the disorientation you feel is not failure—it's transformation in progress.

—Troy Niehaus, Managing Director, Bernstein Private Wealth Management | Major, USAF (Ret.)

I spent twenty-one years at Starbucks learning that it was never about the coffee—it was always about the people. And people don't grow without transformation. Ben Morley understands that truth at a profound level. *Caterpillar Soup at 30,000 Feet* is a courageous and practical guide for any leader willing to do the real work of becoming.

—Howard Behar, former President, Starbucks North America and Starbucks International | Author of *It's Not About the Coffee*

Whether you are a career military person transitioning to the civilian sector or someone trying to advance to the next corporate level, you will not find a better book on how to do both successfully. This book was written by someone I can personally vouch for—having served with him on active duty and someone I don't hesitate to turn to for advice today.

—Danny W. Jessee, E-7, U.S. Navy SEAL (Retired)

What do you do when your world turns upside down? Authors have long found guidance in story and metaphor, such as *Who Moved My Cheese?* or *Our Iceberg Is Melting*. *Caterpillar Soup at 30,000 Feet* takes a fresh approach. It recounts the experiences of a former US Air Force pilot transitioning from Lieutenant Colonel to life after the military, providing a clear roadmap for navigating transformation with clarity and confidence.

This book explores what happens within us during change, clarifies the often confusing path from where you are to where you want to be, and offers tools and language to move forward effectively. More than a one-time read, it is a trusted companion whenever life shifts, helping readers embrace growth with courage and intention.

—Dr. Mark DeVolder, change management speaker and author of *Perpetual Pivot: How the Best Leaders Navigate Exponential Change*

Caterpillar Soup at 30,000 Feet doesn't just leverage the leadership lessons in the military, but also who we become after the lessons. For many great American leaders, military service was just the beginning. Transformation comes from neither rigidly applying military leadership lessons nor abandoning our veteran identities. The metamorphosis involved in becoming an even better leader is not through linear growth but through becoming an entirely different leader with the same DNA, scars, and aspirations.

—John S. Berry, CEO of Berry Law and author of Veteran Led

The best leaders I've known didn't just adapt—they transformed. Ben Morley shows you exactly how to navigate that process and come out the other side stronger."

—Mike Abrashoff, Former Commander USS Benfold | Author of *It's Your Ship*

The decathlon doesn't reward specialists. It demands that you become someone different in each of ten events. Champions aren't built in one discipline—they're forged across all of them. Ben Morley understands that kind of transformation. *Caterpillar Soup at 30,000 Feet* is the playbook for leaders willing to compete across every dimension of who they are.

—Bryan Clay, 2004 Olympic Silver Medalist & 2008 Olympic Gold Medalist, Decathlon | Author of *Redemption*

Ben's book feels like a lifeline for my life's work as a writer. As a fellow traveler who understands the suffocation of self-doubt resulting from lifestyle changes, his insights have helped me dismantle the labels that keep me small. I intend to trade a stagnant routine for the genuine thrill of a new journey—one that will recapture the feeling of a life fueled by purpose and infinite possibility.

—Edie Little, Author of *How Wonder Woman Became a Smuggler*

READ THIS FIRST

Just to say thanks for buying and reading my book,
I would like to connect with you!

Scan the QR Code here.

Caterpillar Soup at 30,000 Feet

The Leader's Guide to Mastering
Your Greatest Transformation

BEN MORLEY

FOREWORD

I've always had a passion for cars. Racing them, stewarding them, appreciating what it takes to build something that performs at the highest level under real-world conditions. One thing I'm learning is that there's a meaningful difference between maintaining a vehicle and truly restoring it. Maintenance keeps things running. Restoration requires you to take the whole thing apart first.

That distinction is at the heart of what Ben Morley has written.

I've had the blessing of working alongside leaders for most of my professional life—first building teams at The Southwestern Company, then founding OneAccord to help Pacific Northwest business owners navigate the most important transitions of their careers, and now stewarding the team and culture at Park Place LTD. What I've seen consistently across all of those contexts is that the leaders who make the greatest impact are rarely the ones who optimized their way to the next level. They're the ones who were willing to be taken apart. Ben and I first crossed paths through KIROS in Bellevue. KIROS exists to help businesspeople make a deeper connection between faith and work, and it tends to attract people who are asking more than surface-level questions about their careers. Ben was one of those people.

He had an impressive record—twenty-seven years in the Air Force, a C-17 instructor pilot, and missions across every continent—but what drew me in was that he wasn't coasting on any of it. He was genuinely grappling with who he was becoming and what personal investment would be necessary to accomplish his goals.

We've stayed in conversation over the years, and I've watched him walk the road he describes in these pages. It wasn't clean or quick. There were seasons of real uncertainty—the kind where the old identity no longer fits, and the new one hasn't fully taken shape. In essence, this describes transformation. He went through the soup. Who has come out is someone more capable, more grounded, and frankly more useful to the people he serves than Lieutenant Colonel Morley ever could have been.

It's a testament to what the process produced.

I've sat with enough owners facing a business sale—commonly the most identity-shaking transition a leader can experience—to know that the external mechanics are rarely the hardest part. It's the internal work. It's recognizing that the version of yourself who built this thing may not be the one meant to carry what comes next. Ben calls that the cocoon phase. I'd call it the most important work a leader can do, and often the most neglected. This book won't make that process comfortable. It will make it navigable. And for many of the leaders—the ones who are too driven to stop, too honest to pretend they've arrived, and too curious to settle—that's precisely what's needed.

Ben didn't write this from a distance. He earned every page.

–Jeff Rogers, Bellevue, Washington
Park Place Ltd
OneAccord
KIROS

Table of Contents

INTRODUCTION

The Altitude of Transformation

30,000 Feet Over the Pacific

I was 30,000 feet over the Pacific Ocean when everything I thought I knew about leadership fell apart.

We had experienced a catastrophic systems failure, the kind that makes your training kick in before your conscious mind even registers what is happening.

My co-pilot looked at me, waiting for the decisive command my rank and experience suggested I should provide, while the crew prepared for whatever orders would follow.

Instead of defaulting to procedures I had executed hundreds of times, I found myself asking a different question: *What is actually happening here that we are not seeing?*

That moment, pausing to see clearly before acting decisively, saved our mission and initiated a transformation in my understanding of leadership, change, and human potential.

This book is about transformation. Not the superficial change that comes from reading business books or attending seminars, but the fundamental change that occurs when you are willing to question who you are and what you are capable of.

The Caterpillar and the Butterfly: A Frame for Everything That Follows

Before we go any further, I want to give you a lens through which every chapter in this book will make more sense. It is a lens drawn not from business school or military doctrine but from one of the most remarkable phenomena in the natural world: the transformation of a caterpillar into a butterfly.

Most people know the broad strokes of the story. A caterpillar passes through four distinct stages of life: egg, caterpillar, pupa, and butterfly. The pupa stage—the biological term for which is chrysalis—is where the most extraordinary and least understood part of the journey takes place. We often see this metamorphosis as a beautiful, gentle process, as nature's way of illustrating that change leads to something better.

What most people do not know is what happens inside that chrysalis.

If you were to open a chrysalis mid-transformation, you would not find a half-formed butterfly. You would find what can best be described as caterpillar soup. The creature has dissolved, its tissues and structures broken down into a biological liquid.

To become a butterfly, the caterpillar must first cease to be a caterpillar, completely and without reservation.

This is the reality of genuine transformation: not refinement, not simple improvement, not optimization, but dissolution. And from that dissolution, something entirely new is assembled from the surviving building blocks of what came before.

I call this the cocooning phase: the withdrawal into that enclosed, transformative space where the old self dissolves and the new self is assembled. It is the central metaphor of this entire book.

The caterpillar doesn't negotiate with the cocoon. It doesn't try to stay partly caterpillar while becoming partly butterfly. It surrenders completely to a process it cannot see or control, and that surrender is the prerequisite for flight.

Everything that follows in these pages is organized around this reality. Each of the nine elements of transformation I will guide you through, including awareness, resistance, identity, fear, letting go, redefinition, forward motion, authenticity, and service, corresponds to a distinct phase of the cocooning experience. Some chapters describe the moment of entering the cocoon. Some describe surviving the dissolution inside it. Some describe the terrifying and exhilarating process of emerging from it.

You may be reading this book because, at some level, you already know you are in one of these phases. You may not have had the language for it yet. Now you will.

Why This Book Exists

After twenty-seven years as a military officer and C-17 instructor pilot, flying missions across all seven continents, I thought I understood transition. I had navigated combat zones, humanitarian crises, and complex international operations, trained dozens of pilots, and led teams through life-and-death situations. Yet when I left the military and entered the civilian world, I experienced something humbling. All that experience had not prepared me for the most challenging transition I would ever face: the shift from the person I had been to the person I was meant to become.

Standing in the parking lot of my first civilian business meeting, with my hands sweating and my heart pounding, I listened to the voice in my head telling me that I did not belong there.

What followed was my personal cocoon phase, that profoundly uncomfortable period when the person I *had been* was dissolving, but the person I *would be* had not yet fully formed. It was messy and uncertain. For months, I felt completely liquefied, unrecognizable to myself, and unsure what would take shape next. I was no longer Lieutenant Colonel Morley, but I had not yet developed the confidence to be Business Consultant Ben.

I questioned whether I had made a tragic mistake, leaving the security of a known identity for the uncertainty of an undefined future. The disorientation, the sleepless nights, the sense of reaching with both hands into darkness and touching nothing—I experienced all of it.

And then something remarkable happened. I emerged, not as a shinier version of Lieutenant Colonel Morley, nor as a military officer who had simply learned to wear business casual, but as something genuinely new. Someone who could bring the depth of twenty-seven years of high-stakes decision-making to the world of business transformation in a way that had never existed before.

That is what the cocoon produces when you trust it: not a slightly better version of what you were, but a fundamentally different expression of what has always been essential in you. This book is the map I wish I had when I was "in the soup."

Who This Book Is For

This book is intended for leaders who sense there is greater impact, deeper alignment, and more of themselves to bring to the table.

You might be an executive who feels a disconnect between the impact you are making and the impact you know you are capable of. You could be a business owner preparing for a major transition like selling your company, bringing in new leadership, or scaling up, realizing that while the technical challenges are manageable, the personal transformation required feels overwhelming.

You may be in mid-career, having achieved everything you thought you wanted, only to find that it does not feel as you expected. Alternatively, you might be facing an involuntary transition like having your position eliminated, experiencing company acquisitions, or confronting market disruptions, and now you must redefine who you are when your old identity no longer fits.

Perhaps you are not officially in a leadership role but are still leading your own life through significant change and need frameworks to navigate uncertainty with courage rather than becoming paralyzed by it.

If you have picked up this book, you likely sense that the next chapter of your life will require more than new skills or strategies. It will require a transformation in how you see yourself, make decisions, and engage with the world. In other words, you may already be in your cocoon. You just didn't know what to call it.

What Makes This Book Different

This is not another guide to goal-setting, productivity hacks, or leadership competencies. It focuses on the internal work that makes external success sustainable and meaningful.

It explores the transformation that occurs not in conference rooms or strategic planning sessions but in the uncomfortable space between who you have been and who you are becoming. That space—the cocoon—is where this book lives.

Most leadership books focus on the caterpillar phase, optimizing your current capabilities, or the butterfly phase, which is what a fully transformed leader looks like. Almost none address the cocoon itself or the disorienting middle where real transformation occurs. This book is about the cocoon.

The frameworks presented here originate from three key sources:

First, my twenty-seven years of military aviation experience, where the stakes were often life and death. The lessons learned about awareness, decision-making under pressure, and crisis leadership were forged under real-world conditions that cannot be replicated in a classroom.

Second, my years of consulting with Fortune 500 companies and business owners during major transitions have allowed me to observe what truly works when leaders and organizations face complex challenges that do not have textbook solutions.

Third, I draw from my own transformative journey, transitioning from a military officer to a civilian consultant, moving from an identity entwined with rank and role to discovering who I truly am beneath that structure. I have been the caterpillar. I have been the soup. I have been the butterfly. And I have walked alongside hundreds of leaders through every phase of that process.

I am not writing as someone who has it all figured out, but as someone who has walked this path, made many mistakes, and identified principles that genuinely help when you are navigating transformation without a clear roadmap.

The Journey Ahead: Nine Phases of the Cocoon

This book is organized around nine critical elements of transformation, each building upon the last. Together, they trace the complete arc of the cocoon experience, from the moment you sense that your current form no longer fits, through the dissolution in the middle, to the emergence of something new.

- **Awareness** is where all transformation begins, the moment the caterpillar first senses the cocoon calling. You cannot change what you cannot see clearly. In this element, you will develop situational awareness that helps you to notice patterns others miss and recognize the gap between your current reality and your potential.

- **Resistance** arises as soon as awareness increases: the instinct to keep crawling rather than surrender to the cocoon. Your mind launches a sophisticated campaign to dissuade you from acting on what you see. You will learn to recognize resistance in its many forms and work with it rather than be paralyzed by it.

- **Identity** involves a deep examination of who you are beyond your role, title, or position, and it is a necessary reckoning before dissolution can begin. You will differentiate between the personas you have constructed to meet external expectations and the authentic self that exists beneath that conditioning.

- **Fear** stands as a guardian at the gate of your next level; it's what you feel at the entrance to your cocoon. You will distinguish between useful caution and paralyzing anxiety and build the courage to act in the presence of fear instead of waiting for it to disappear.

- **Letting Go** is the strategic release of patterns, beliefs, and identities that no longer serve the person you are becoming, entering the cocoon and allowing the dissolution to begin. You will explore why this is so challenging and how to release what no longer serves you.

- **Redefinition** is the intentional work of becoming who you were meant to be, the reorganization of surviving essence into a new form. You will integrate the best of your past self with the person you are becoming, moving beyond linear thinking into the complex reality of genuine growth.

- **Forward Motion** is where insight transforms into action, the first movements of newly formed wings. You will explore the difference between goals and plans, learn to start with zero rather than simply improving existing complex systems, and develop the capacity for sustainable progress.

- **Authenticity** is the courage to be yourself, even when it's inconvenient, emerging from the cocoon, even when others prefer the caterpillar. You will see why authenticity is not only more fulfilling than performance but also more effective.

- **Service** is the ultimate expression of transformed capability, the butterfly taking flight in the service of something greater than itself. You will discover how your authentic gifts, aligned with genuine needs, create value that far exceeds your original intentions.

You don't need to memorize these now. As we move through the chapters, you will begin to recognize these elements in your own story.

How To Use This Book

You can read this book from cover to cover, which is probably the most effective approach for your first time through. The chapters build on one another, with concepts introduced early becoming the foundation for frameworks presented later.

However, transformation is not linear. You may find yourself revisiting specific chapters as different elements become relevant at different stages. You might need to return to Chapter 2 on resistance multiple times, as you encounter it in new forms. Similarly, you may revisit Chapter 3 on identity, as new layers of self-understanding emerge.

Each chapter of this book includes stories from my military experience, consulting work, and personal transformation. These stories are not just illustrations; they are the fundamental material from which the principles emerged. Pay close attention to the stories that resonate with you, as they often point toward something important you need to hear.

You will also find frameworks and questions designed to help you apply these concepts to your own situation. Take the time to engage with them; transformation is not a spectator sport.

A Word About Timing

If you are reading this book, you are likely in the midst of a transition or about to undergo one. This is not a coincidence. We typically seek resources when we need them, not before.

Here is what I want you to understand: wherever you are in your journey right now is exactly where you are meant to be. If you find yourself in the messy middle of a major transition, feeling like everything is falling apart, know that this is not evidence of failure. It is evidence that you are in your cocoon and that real transformation is occurring.

The caterpillar does not experience the dissolution as beautiful. It simply experiences it. What allows it to complete the process is not certainty about the outcome, comfort with the process, or even an understanding of what is happening. The caterpillar completes the process because it cannot stop the process once it has begun.

You are reading this book because something in you has already begun, and that awareness is valuable. Something essential is already dissolving, and something new is assembling in the darkness. Your job is not to stop the process or rush it, but to understand it well enough to trust it.

If you haven't started your transition yet but sense that change is on the horizon, this gives you the opportunity to prepare in a way you wouldn't be able to if change took you by surprise.

If you are on the other side of a significant transition, looking back and trying to make sense of your experiences, this book can help you understand what you have been through and integrate those lessons in ways that will support your continued growth.

The caterpillar doesn't know it's going to become a butterfly; it simply experiences the uncertainty of its transformation. That sense of dissolution is not failure or a detour. It is the main event.

The Invitation

This book serves as an invitation to stop living reactively and start living authentically, rather than conforming to someone else's definition of success, and to create your own based on who you genuinely are and what you are capable of contributing.

It is an invitation to see clearly, act courageously, and serve meaningfully. It calls you to do the difficult work of transformation, to enter your cocoon willingly, to trust the dissolution, and to remain committed to the process even when you cannot yet see what is being assembled.

The caterpillar has no guarantee of flight. It surrenders to the process anyway. That surrender—that willingness to dissolve completely in service of becoming—is the bravest thing any of us will ever do.

The world needs what you have to offer. Your unique combination of experience, perspective, values, and capabilities only emerges when you stop protecting the caterpillar and trust the cocoon.

Are you ready to begin?

Every transformation begins with a single moment of honest seeing, the instant the caterpillar first senses the cocoon calling. In the chapter that follows, we start there: with awareness and the story of a flight that taught me why seeing clearly is the foundation for everything else.

CHAPTER 1

Awareness—The Foundation of All Transformation

Let me begin with a story from my days as a C-17 pilot that fundamentally changed how I perceive awareness.

We were on a mission to a remote airfield, the kind of place where you only get one chance at the approach. We had no radar and no backup systems.

My co-pilot was relatively new. As we descended through the clouds, I sensed that something was off. The wind patterns did not match what we had been briefed on during mission planning.

The visual cues from the ground looked different from what was expected. However, my co-pilot was fixated on his instruments, following the approach as briefed and completely unaware of these subtle signs.

"What do you see out there?" I asked him. He rattled off the standard information: airspeed, altitude, heading. All correct. But he wasn't seeing what I was seeing.

He was not picking up on the signs that revealed the true situation of our environment. That moment made me realize that the difference between good pilots and great pilots lies not only in technical skill but also in awareness, the ability to recognize patterns, read situations, and notice signals that others completely miss.

This principle applies whether you're leading a company, navigating a career transition, or making critical business decisions. The most successful leaders I have worked with, ranging from Fortune 500 C-suite executives to small business owners preparing for mergers and acquisitions, all share the same superpower: exceptional situational awareness.

ACTION STEP: Develop Your Situational Awareness

→ In your next meeting or site visit, set one rule: spend the first five minutes only observing without talking or using devices.

→ Ask yourself: *What is everyone paying attention to? What is no one paying attention to?*

→ After the meeting, write down two things you noticed that were not on the official agenda.

→ Over time, build a habit of asking: *What would a first-time observer see here that I no longer notice?*

→ The gap between what you see and what others see is your awareness advantage.

What Tracking Taught Me About Life

A few years ago, I encountered the work of Boyd Varty, a wildlife tracker from South Africa who runs a game reserve. Boyd uses the ancient art of tracking big game animals and applies those principles to discovering purpose in life. His teachings revolutionized my understanding of awareness.

Boyd explained that the first step to tracking a lion in the wild is to become very comfortable with uncertainty. You must abandon all your preconceived notions of knowing what to do and instead embrace the mindset of "I do not know how to do this."

Many leaders find themselves in a challenging position during major transitions. When I left my twenty-seven-year career in the Air Force, I thought I knew my identity. I was Lieutenant Colonel Ben Morley, a C-17 instructor pilot and director of operations. But that was what I did, not who I was.

As a young tracker learning the art, Boyd would be sent down a trail and told to report his observations. Initially, he would mention only a herd of impala crossing the path.

His instructor urged him to try again, this time looking and observing like an animal, with his head lowered close to the trail. On subsequent trips down the same path, he discovered layers of information he had missed. Yes, the impala had crossed, but they had also walked over leopard tracks. He started to notice where a mouse had scurried across the path and where an owl had swooped down, touching the ground with its wing. Each time he walked that trail, he uncovered more information, but only if he was attuned to see it.

This is exactly what I teach executives when they prepare for significant business transitions or exit strategies. There is valuable information within your organization, in your market, and within yourself, but you must learn to be attuned to it.

What do you need to focus on during transformational processes? Consider the things that make you feel expansive and alive. Let go of your rigid ideas about what you should do and pay attention to what draws you in. Notice what piques your curiosity and the activities that consistently energize you.

ACTION STEP: Walk the Trail Again

→ Choose one area of your business or life that feels stuck or familiar: a team dynamic, a recurring problem, or a market you think you understand.

→ Approach it as a first-time tracker: set aside what you already "know" and look for what is actually there, then ask three-layered questions, moving from obvious to subtle:

- *What is the most visible thing happening here?*
- *What is happening underneath, in the relationships, the culture, the unspoken dynamics?*
- *What is the smallest signal—the mouse track, the owl's wing—that points to something larger?*

→ The information you have been missing is usually already present. You just haven't been attuned to see it.

Three Hundred Shades of Green

The World Economic Forum has identified the most important skills for the future. Among these are complex problem-solving, critical thinking, and creativity. If you possess these skills, you are precisely what the world needs, even in this era of artificial intelligence. Organizations are seeking leaders who embody these skills.

Let's look at what constitutes a complex problem. The term "complex" refers to a problem that has many different moving parts or components. It can be confusing, contradictory, knotted up, and tangled, like the roots of a tree. Some complex problems we all currently face include global warming, terrorism, mental health, and microplastics in our food supply. These are not simple or ordinary problems. The world is looking for people who are not intimidated or afraid of problems of this nature and are willing to develop the skills to handle complexity rather than avoid it.

To explain, I present to you the importance of nuance. "Nuance" comes from the French word for "shade," pointing to subtle gradations rather than blunt categories. Navigating complexity, both personally and professionally, demands that we become comfortable with nuance and open ourselves to various viewpoints rather than sticking to our learned ways of thinking.

I learned this lesson the hard way during my transition from military to civilian leadership. In the Air Force, we operated within clear hierarchies, established procedures, and defined outcomes. However, in the business world, particularly when working with family-owned companies preparing for sale or assisting C-suite leaders with organizational change, there are often multiple valid perspectives, and each situation has nuance.

Tyranny is the deliberate removal of nuance. When I deny you a shade different from mine or disregard a different perspective or opinion, I demonstrate an inability to engage in complex problem-solving, becoming narrow-minded and fixed in my viewpoint.

This leads me to the color green. Do you like the color green? If so, which one?

There are nearly three hundred shades of green, including various hues of lime green and countless versions of forest green, emerald, sage, and mint. Although they all fall under the umbrella of "green," there are distinct differences, even in their Pantone shades.

To digress for a moment, scientists have determined that the average human eye can distinguish roughly a million different colors, and some people can see many times that number. In practical terms, that means there are hundreds of distinct shades of green your brain can perceive, even if you do not have names for them.

That's an astonishing number of shades of green!

Remember the internet dress phenomenon? Was the dress white and gold or blue and black? People who perceived it one way found it hard to believe that others saw it differently. This phenomenon occurs because our eye receptors interpret colors in varying ways.

This variability in perception exemplifies what complex problem-solving entails. It requires a willingness to appreciate differing perspectives without resorting to conflict over whose viewpoint is correct.

ACTION STEP: Develop Your Range of Perception

→ In your next complex decision or conflict, before forming a conclusion, deliberately seek out two perspectives you have not yet considered.

→ Seek someone out who disagrees with the prevailing view and ask them to help you understand how they see it. Listen without preparing your rebuttal.

→ Notice your physical response when someone's viewpoint conflicts with yours. That tension is your nuance threshold, the edge of your current perception.

→ Practice the "shades" question. Instead of asking, "Do I agree or disagree?" ask, "What shade of truth does this perspective hold?"

→ Complex problem-solving, critical thinking, and creativity all begin with the willingness to see more than one color.

Chess vs. Checkers Players

In my work with leadership teams, I often share a metaphor: Great leaders play chess, not checkers.

In checkers, all the pieces are identical, have the same value, and move in essentially one direction. In chess, however, each piece has a distinct value and unique capabilities. A pawn moves differently from a knight, and a bishop moves differently from a rook. As Bobby Fischer, the former world chess champion, put it, "Winning in chess is all about understanding how to capitalize on the strengths of each piece and timing their moves just right."

This is the essence of great leadership. You cannot achieve the best outcomes from individuals by playing checkers with people or expecting the same results from each person, as if they were interchangeable parts in a system. Throughout my years leading operations teams and training pilots, I learned that every person has a unique way of thinking, building relationships, learning, and processing information.

The best leaders discover what is unique about each person and leverage that uniqueness. To lead effectively, you must recognize four key qualities in others: strengths and weaknesses, triggers, personality, and learning styles.

1. Strengths & Weaknesses

Connect with people through their strengths. Identify the weaknesses that drain their energy, as well as the strong points where they consistently thrive. Deploy them in ways that align with their best work.

2. Triggers

Understand what motivates each team member. Is it verbal praise, time spent with the leader, more autonomy, or opportunities for growth and challenge? Each individual has different motivational triggers, and knowing them gives you leverage as a leader.

3. Personality

Be aware of the personality differences within your team. Are team members more analytical, relationship-driven, or results-oriented? Recognizing these differences and adjusting how you communicate and make decisions can significantly enhance your leadership effectiveness.

4. Learning Style

Determine how each person learns best. Do they assimilate by studying and analyzing, by diving in and doing, or by observing others? Tailoring your approach to match their learning styles accelerates development.

I have witnessed how these principles can transform organizations. When I assist companies preparing for mergers and acquisitions (M&A), one of the first evaluations is whether leadership is playing chess or checkers with their team. The organizations that receive the highest evaluations are the ones where leaders have intentionally nurtured each individual according to their unique strengths.

ACTION STEP: Play Chess with Your Team

→ Choose one person on your team and work through the four dimensions introduced in this section:

- **Strengths & Weaknesses:** What tasks consistently energize this person? What drains them? Are you deploying them accordingly?
- **Triggers:** What does this person respond to most? Praise? Autonomy? Challenge? Growth opportunities? Have you ever asked them directly?
- **Personality:** Does this person prefer to operate through analysis, relationships, or results? Does your leadership style currently meet them where they are?
- **Learning Style:** Does this person learn best by studying, doing, or watching? Is the development you offer matched to how they actually absorb information?

→ Repeat this exercise for every member of your team. The leaders who score highest in M&A evaluations and build the strongest cultures are the ones who can answer these questions for every person they lead.

The Pattern Recognition Breakthrough

My own awareness breakthrough occurred during a consulting project with a manufacturing company struggling with persistent quality issues. They had brought in multiple consultants before me, each focusing on different technical solutions such as equipment upgrades, process modifications, and training programs.

But within the first week of observation, I noticed something unrelated to their manufacturing processes. I saw patterns in how the leadership team communicated during shift changes. There were information gaps, unclear handoffs, and what is referred to in aviation as "authority gradient" issues, meaning junior employees weren't comfortable speaking up when they noticed problems.

Everyone else was looking at the machinery. I was watching the human systems, the non-technical skills that ensure all team members can contribute effectively to safety and mission success, knowing that poor communication kills more flights than mechanical failure ever will.

When I presented this to the leadership team, the plant manager initially resisted. "We've tried communication training," he said. "Our problem is technical, not interpersonal."

But awareness has taught me that the real problem is usually not what people think it is. The technical issues were symptoms. The communication patterns were the root cause.

Something shifted during our second week together. I asked the plant manager to walk the floor with me during a shift change, not to inspect equipment but simply to observe. We stood quietly near the handoff between the outgoing and incoming supervisors. The exchange lasted less than two minutes. Critical information about a recurring pressure variance on Line 3 was mentioned once, in passing, then lost in the noise of the transition.

"Did you catch that?" I asked him afterward.

He had not.

I showed him data I'd been quietly collecting, not defect rates, which he knew by heart, but communication patterns. How often operators flagged concerns verbally versus in writing, and how frequently those concerns made it from the floor to his desk. The gap between the two numbers was significant.

He was quiet for a long moment. "So the equipment isn't lying to us," he finally said. "We just can't hear it."

That was the opening. Not an argument won, but a problem reframed in terms he could own.

We implemented crew resource management principles adapted for manufacturing. We created structured communication protocols for shift handoffs. We established psychological safety so operators could voice concerns without fear of blame.

The result? Quality defects dropped by 73 percent in six months. Not because we upgraded equipment or modified processes, but because we enabled the team to see and communicate about problems before they became defects.

That's when I understood that developing awareness isn't just about seeing what's there but about seeing what others miss. It's about recognizing patterns that connect seemingly unrelated phenomena and understanding that the most important information is often hiding in plain sight.

ACTION STEP: Find the Root Cause, Not the Symptom

→ Identify one persistent problem in your organization that has resisted repeated technical fixes.

→ Temporarily set aside the technical layer and examine the human system underneath:

- How is information flowing (or not flowing) between people and teams?
- Where are the handoff points? What gets lost or distorted at each transition?
- Who is not speaking up, and why? What does the authority gradient look like?

→ Ask: *If the machinery (process, system, tool) were perfect, would this problem still exist?* If the answer is yes, the root cause is human, not technical.

→ The most important information is usually hiding in plain sight in the conversations that aren't happening.

Awareness in Action

Awareness provides moments of clarity that prevent us from returning to unconscious living. This is what I refer to as "awareness in action." In my consulting work, I observe leaders at various stages of this journey toward awareness.

Some leaders are just beginning to recognize the gap between their current reality and their potential. Others are deeply engaged in major transitions, whether they are preparing their companies for sale, navigating post-acquisition integration, or stepping into higher levels of leadership responsibility. Regardless of their stage, the pattern remains constant.

Awareness must come first; you need to see clearly before you can act effectively. Whether I'm coaching an executive through a critical decision, assisting a leadership team in optimizing their operational processes, or helping business owners enhance their enterprise value before a transaction, everything begins with awareness.

This includes awareness of current market dynamics, understanding their team's actual capabilities rather than mere assumptions, and recognizing the gap between existing systems and what potential buyers expect.

Most importantly, it involves self-awareness, understanding who you are beyond your current role, and recognizing what you're genuinely capable of achieving when you stop confining yourself to old definitions.

Self-awareness is akin to having a drone observing you from above. While many people might be self-conscious, fewer cultivate true self-awareness.

The Foundation for Everything

This concept serves as the foundation for everything I have learned through my experiences on seven continents, leading teams through high-stakes operations, and guiding numerous leaders through significant transitions. Awareness is essential to everything that follows.

You can only transform what you can see clearly. Effective leadership requires an understanding of the unique value each individual brings. Making sound decisions under pressure hinges on your situational awareness.

Navigating complex transitions demands that you comprehend both your current position and your potential future path. Awareness, it turns out, has a cost. The moment you begin to see clearly, something in you will fight to look away. That fight has a name, and learning to recognize it is the only way through. Once you achieve this level of awareness and begin to see clearly, you cannot return to unconscious living.

You become aware of the gap between your current reality and your potential, and this awareness can create resistance. Your mind may wish to return to the comfortable illusion that everything is fine the way it was.

Your environment might resist the changes that this awareness demands. The people around you might prefer the previous version of you, one that was more predictable and controllable. This resistance is where many people get stuck.

They develop awareness but then allow resistance to prevent them from acting on what they perceive. In the next chapter, we will explore how to recognize and work with that resistance instead of allowing it to stop you. Because awareness without action is simply sophisticated procrastination.

The question is not whether you have the ability to see more clearly. The real question is whether you are willing to act on what you observe, even when those actions feel uncertain, uncomfortable, or risky.

This is where true transformation begins.

REFLECTION: Turn Awareness into Action

Run a four-domain awareness audit before moving to the next chapter:

→ Market: What is changing in your competitive environment that you have been slow to acknowledge?

→ Team: What do you assume about your team's capabilities that you have not recently verified?

→ Systems: Where is there a gap between how your organization currently operates and what the next level demands?

→ Self: Who are you beyond your current title? What are you genuinely capable of that your current role does not yet require?

→ Write one honest answer for each domain. These are not problems to solve right now, but they are things to see clearly.

→ Awareness without action is sophisticated procrastination. The next chapter will show you what to do with what you now see.

CHAPTER 2

Resistance—When Your Mind Fights Back

I was sitting in my rental car in the parking lot of my client's office in Dallas, Texas, staring at the building where I was about to attend my first business meeting as a civilian consultant.

After twenty-seven years of military service, I was now expected to be an expert in operational excellence and business strategy. My hands were sweating, my heart was pounding, and the voice in my head was relentless. *What are you doing here? These are real business leaders. They have MBAs. They have built companies. You flew airplanes. You do not belong in this room.*

I had just left a career where I was respected, where I knew my role, and where people looked to me for leadership in life-or-death situations. I had trained pilots, led international operations, and managed multimillion-dollar budgets, but sitting in that parking lot, none of that mattered. All I could hear was the voice telling me I was about to be exposed as a fraud.

What I didn't understand then was that I was experiencing one of the most predictable responses to increased self-awareness. The moment you start seeing clearly, when you recognize the gap between where you are and where you could be, your mind launches a sophisticated campaign to talk you out of taking any action. This is resistance, and it's where most transformation stalls.

ACTION STEP: Recognize Resistance in Real Time

→ The next time hesitation strikes before a high-stakes moment, pause and name it: "This is resistance."

→ Ask yourself: *Is this a genuine warning, or is my mind trying to keep me small?*

→ Write down the answer. Seeing it on paper exposes how often it is distortion, not data.

→ Remind yourself that resistance rises most sharply right before breakthroughs.

The Many Faces of Resistance

Resistance often disguises itself, rarely announcing its true intent. Instead of introducing itself with a name tag that says, "Hi, I'm here to sabotage your growth," it appears as legitimate concerns, practical considerations, and rational thinking. Resistance is a shape-shifter.

Let me share an experience from my pilot training that illustrated how resistance operates in real time. I was flying a navigational exercise known as "fix-to-fix" in a T-37 jet. We did not use GPS, so I relied solely on the steam gauges and one navigational aid to guide me into a holding pattern.

This technique was notorious for being stressful. As I approached the fix, I found myself constantly second-guessing my decisions. *Should I update my heading? Had the wind pushed me off course?* When I finally arrived and turned to enter the holding pattern, I immediately began to doubt whether I had turned in the correct direction. Did I turn the wrong way?

As it turned out, I *had* turned the wrong way, and I was sure I had just failed this flight. I was in disbelief. I was frustrated and angry with myself because I would have to repeat the entire flight and likely fall behind in my training.

While this internal dialogue was spiraling out of control, I still needed to focus on flying the airplane. I wasn't finished with my flight; I had an instrument approach to complete. However, my mind was stuck replaying what I thought was a mistake, preventing me from executing the next phase of the mission. Later, I discovered that I hadn't actually turned the wrong direction and hadn't failed anything. However, I almost failed the subsequent approach because I was so hung up on what I mistakenly believed to be an error.

This illustrates how resistance works. It can keep you so focused on replaying past mistakes or worrying about future failures that you become unable to stay present and accomplish what is in front of you. Flight instructors referred to this as "compartmentalization failure," which is the inability to set aside one issue and concentrate on the current task. This was one of the most common reasons students failed to progress through pilot training.

ACTION STEP: Stay Present When It Matters Most

→ When your mind starts replaying a setback in the middle of an important task, catch the drift and interrupt it.

→ Ask: *Is the current mission finished?* If not, your only job right now is to complete it.

→ Bring your attention to the immediate next action. What do the next five minutes require of me?

→ Reserve your self-evaluation for after the task is complete. Analyzing mid-flight costs you the approach.

The Creativity Killer

Estimates suggest that a majority of people, often cited as around 70 percent, experience imposter syndrome feelings at least once in their lives. If you've experienced this feeling, you are not alone; you are actually part of the majority, especially among high achievers, leaders, and individuals navigating significant transitions.

However, imposter syndrome is just one manifestation of resistance. There are others, and they all serve the same purpose: to prevent you from expressing your authentic capabilities.

Creativity is the opposite of helplessness. When you engage in creative activities, when you build something new, and when you venture into uncharted territory, you assert your self-sovereignty.

You might say, "I do not have to accept the limitations that others have placed on me or that I have placed on myself." However, resistance often emerges to protect you from the vulnerability that comes with putting yourself out there. The ego, essentially resistance dressed up in a fancy outfit, acts as creativity's bodyguard. Its role is to safeguard your identity. The issue is that the identity the ego protects is often false.

When I walked into that business meeting in Dallas, my ego was working overtime. It was trying to defend the identity of a "successful Air Force officer" by preventing me from risking failure as an "inexperienced business consultant." My ego preferred that I remain in a comfortable, limited identity rather than risk the growth that would come with expansion.

Resistance whispers thoughts like, *Don't do that. Don't be vulnerable. Don't share that idea. Don't offer that insight. What if they think you are not qualified? What if they ask you something you cannot answer?* As a result, you remain silent. You don't share the insight that could transform their business. You don't propose the solution that seems obvious to you because of your unique background. You don't step into the full expression of your capabilities because resistance has convinced you that safety lies in staying small.

ACTION STEP: Reclaim Your Creativity

→ Identify one insight, idea, or solution you have been withholding out of fear of judgment.

→ Ask: *What is the cost, to others, of my staying silent?* Let the answer motivate action.

→ Share the idea in its smallest viable form: a sentence, a note, or a question in a meeting.

→ Track the actual outcome versus what resistance predicted. Let the evidence expose resistance as the liar it is.

The Legitimate Disguises

Here's what makes resistance so effective: It disguises itself as genuine excuses and legitimate reasons for not moving forward.

You might think, *I am not ready yet.* But being ready is overrated. You will never feel completely prepared for the next level of challenge. If you wait until you feel ready, you will wait forever.

Perhaps you tell yourself, *I do not have enough resources.* I have seen organizations achieve extraordinary things with minimal resources, while others with abundant resources accomplished nothing. The key difference was not the resources but resourcefulness.

You might also think, *I am not qualified.* Qualified compared to whom? Most of the people doing what you aspire to were not "qualified" when they started, either; they became qualified by putting in the work.

Another excuse could be, *It is not the right time.* However, there is never a perfect time. The only time that matters is when you decide to stop waiting for permission from circumstances and start creating the circumstances you need.

You might also believe that you do not live in the right place or do not have the right connections. All of these thoughts contribute to the internal chatter that creates resistance to taking action.

Sometimes, resistance shows up disguised as your current circumstances. Divorce, health issues, and family challenges are real and require attention, but they can also become reasons to postpone growth indefinitely.

Often, the best creativity, breakthroughs, and achievements emerge from difficult circumstances. Top athletes frequently perform while dealing with injuries. Sometimes, you must create while healing, build while processing, and move forward while facing challenges.

ACTION STEP: Unmask the Legitimate Excuses

→ List every reason you are currently not moving forward on a key goal.

→ Next to each item below, answer: Is this a real barrier or resistance in disguise?

Replace the excuse with a resourceful question:

→ Not ready → What minimum preparation lets me take one step today?

→ No resources → What can I do with what I already have?

→ Not qualified → Who started without full qualifications and succeeded anyway?

→ Wrong timing → What one action, taken now, would create better timing?

→ Bad circumstances → What have others created from circumstances harder than mine?

The Business Meeting Breakthrough

Let's go back to that parking lot. I'm sitting in the car, sweating, and listening to my internal resistance, which is debating whether I should just drive back to the hotel and pretend the meeting got canceled. Then, I recalled something from my military training. In aviation, we say, "It's not over until you are safe on the ground, the engines are off, and the chocks are in."

I was still on a mission, and that mission was not to feel confident; it was to serve the client by offering my unique perspective and capabilities to their challenges.

So, I made a decision: I would not try to be someone I was not. I wouldn't pretend to have an MBA or twenty years of corporate experience. I would show up as myself, someone who had led teams through high-stakes operations, understood systems and processes, and could see problems from angles that traditional business consultants might miss.

When I walked into that meeting as my true self, something interesting happened. Instead of being exposed as a fraud, I was able to offer insights that no one else in the room had considered. My military background wasn't a liability; it was a differentiator.

The client was facing a quality-control issue costing them hundreds of thousands of dollars annually. While the business consultants in the room approached the problem with traditional frameworks, I viewed it through the lens of operational risk management, something we worked with every day in aviation.

Within an hour, we identified the root cause and developed a solution that not only addressed their immediate problem but also prevented similar issues across their operation. The changes resulted in more than a million dollars in cost savings. None of this would have happened if I had listened to my resistance.

ACTION STEP: Lead with Your Differentiator

→ Before your next high-stakes meeting or presentation, write down three things your unique background gives you that others in the room do not have.

→ Reframe your "liabilities" as assets. What does your non-traditional path reveal that insiders miss?

→ Set a mission statement for the event, not about how you will feel, but about the value you will deliver.

→ After the meeting, note what actually happened versus what resistance predicted. Use that data next time.

The Management Strategy

Resistance is not something you can eliminate. It is something you manage. Even the most successful individuals I know, including CEOs, world-class athletes, and accomplished artists, still encounter resistance. The difference is that they have learned to recognize it and work with it rather than succumb to its paralysis.

First, learn to identify resistance for what it is. When you are about to do something that could expand your capabilities or impact, or when you are about to step into a greater version of yourself, resistance will arise. Anticipate it. In fact, it's a good sign. It indicates that you are moving in the right direction.

Second, understand that resistance often becomes louder just before breakthroughs. The closer you get to stepping into your authentic power, the more sophisticated resistance will become. It will pull out all the stops to keep you in your comfort zone.

Third, develop what I call "present moment awareness." When resistance causes you to replay past failures or rehearse future disasters, redirect your attention back to the present. Focus on what the next right action is and what needs your attention right now.

In my consulting work, I frequently observe this pattern. Leaders on the verge of significant breakthroughs often experience the most intense resistance. Business owners preparing for M&A suddenly question their readiness. Executives stepping into new roles doubt their qualifications. High-performing teams facing new challenges worry they lack the necessary skills. The key is to learn to act in the presence of resistance rather than waiting for it to dissipate.

ACTION STEP: Build Your Resistance Management System

Step 1: Identify: Create a personal "resistance signature."

→ What form does your resistance usually take? Procrastination? Over-preparation? Sudden busyness? Awareness is the first line of defense.

Step 2: Anticipate: Pre-brief your resistance.

→ Before big moments, tell yourself: *Resistance will show up here. That's expected, and it means I'm on the right track.*

Step 3: Act anyway: Use a minimum viable action.

→ Commit to the smallest possible action that moves you forward, be it a single email, a five-minute start, or one phone call. Momentum defeats resistance.

The Compartmentalization Skill

Remember that time during my flight when I almost failed the approach because I was mentally stuck in a holding pattern? That experience taught me one of the most valuable skills for dealing with resistance: how to compartmentalize effectively.

Mistake analysis is best conducted on stable ground after the mission is complete, at 1G and zero knots, as we like to say. When you are in the middle of executing a task, you must set aside self-doubt and focus on what needs to be done.

This principle directly applies to business and leadership situations. For example, if you are delivering an important presentation and stumble over a word, resistance will want you to spend the next ten minutes replaying that mistake and worrying about what the audience thinks. However, the presentation isn't over, and you still have value to deliver.

Similarly, if you are leading a team through a challenging project and make a decision that doesn't turn out perfectly, resistance will prompt you to second-guess every subsequent decision. Yet, the project isn't finished, and your team still needs clear leadership.

If you are in negotiations for a major business transaction and something does not go as planned, resistance tries to urge you to catastrophize and think that the entire deal is collapsing. However, you are still in the negotiation process.

There are still options available to you, and the key is to say: *I will process this later. Right now, I need to focus on what is in front of me.*

ACTION STEP: Master the Compartmentalization Toolkit

The 1G/Zero Knots Rule:

→ Mistake analysis belongs on the ground after the mission is complete. Never conduct your debrief mid-flight.

→ When self-doubt surfaces during execution, say: *I will process this later. Right now, I need to focus on what is in front of me.*

The Three-Second Present-Moment Reset:

→ Name it: *My mind just left the mission.*

→ Ground it: Take one slow breath and feel both feet on the floor.

→ Redirect it: Ask, *What is the most important action in the next five minutes?*

The Resistance Paradox

The paradox of resistance is that the very things it tries to protect you from are often the experiences you need for growth. For instance, it attempts to shield you from failure, but failure is essential for learning. It aims to protect you from rejection, yet putting yourself out there is how you find the right opportunities. It tries to guard you against uncertainty, but uncertainty is where possibility resides.

In my work with leadership teams, I've observed that the most innovative solutions often arise from individuals who initially resist change. Once they work through their resistance, they often become the strongest advocates for transformation. I reflect on the executives I've coached who initially feared stepping into larger roles, only to discover capabilities they didn't know they possessed.

I think of the business owners who felt paralyzed by the complexity of preparing for sale, yet ultimately navigated transactions that transformed their lives. There are also the operational teams that believed they couldn't improve their efficiency but went on to achieve breakthrough results. The resistance they felt was not evidence of incapability; it was a sign that they were about to expand beyond their current identity.

KEY INSIGHT: Use Resistance as a Compass

→ Resistance is not a stop sign but a directional signal pointing toward growth.

→ The stronger the resistance, the closer you likely are to a significant breakthrough.

The Creative Courage

Creativity requires courage, a fact often overlooked. Courage is not the absence of fear or resistance; it is the willingness to feel fear and resistance and choose to act anyway.

The courage you find to be creative and step into your next self may lead to unforeseen consequences, consequences that are often positive. Consider the lives you can impact, the value you can create, and the problems you can solve when you stop allowing resistance to keep you small.

I recall the business owners who overcame their resistance to implement operational improvements. Not only did they increase their company's value, but they also created better working conditions for their employees. Their courage to act despite uncertainty had a ripple effect, benefiting dozens, if not hundreds, of people.

I also recall executives who pushed past imposter syndrome to embrace leadership roles they initially believed they weren't qualified for. They not only experienced personal growth but also became the leaders their organizations desperately needed.

Your resistance isn't just about you; it extends to everyone around you. When you allow resistance to win, you not only limit yourself but also restrict your potential contributions to others.

REFLECTION: Your Resistance Affects Others

→ Write down the names of three people who would benefit if you stepped fully into your potential.

→ For each person, describe one specific way your growth would positively impact them.

→ Read this list before any high-resistance moment. Courage expands when the mission is larger than yourself.

→ Ask: *Who am I holding back by staying small?* Let that answer fuel your next step.

The Bridge to Identity

I've learned that resistance often signifies that you are outgrowing your current identity. The person you've been cannot fulfill the requirements of the person you are becoming. Resistance, then, is the friction between these two identities.

For example, the identity of "Air Force pilot Ben" could not confidently walk into a business meeting. That identity was too narrow for the contribution I felt called to make. In contrast, "Leadership Consultant Ben" was able to combine military operational experience with business challenges, enabling him to offer unique value. The resistance I experienced wasn't merely fear; it was the labor pains of a new identity being born.

Resistance, it turns out, is not really about the situation in front of you. It is about the identity behind you, the one that cannot yet imagine surviving what comes next. Before you can move through resistance for good, you have to ask a harder question: *Who am I, really, when the uniform comes off?*

You cannot become someone you are not already. The person you are meant to be is not out there waiting to be discovered; that individual is already within you, waiting to be revealed, expressed, and given permission to emerge.

However, to uncover this true self, you must be willing to question everything you think you know about who you are.

CHAPTER 3

Identity—Who You Are Beyond What You Do

The letter arrived on a Tuesday morning in March. After twenty-seven years of military service, it was official: Lieutenant Colonel Benjamin Morley was retiring from the United States Air Force.

I stared at that piece of paper for a long time. During my time, I had progressed from second lieutenant to lieutenant colonel, from student pilot to instructor pilot, and eventually to mission commander.

I had landed on all seven continents, led teams through life-and-death operations, managed multimillion-dollar budgets, and trained dozens of pilots. But as I sat there with that retirement letter, I realized something that shook me to my core: I had no idea who I was without my uniform.

For nearly three decades, when someone asked who I was, the answer was simple: I am an Air Force pilot. It wasn't just what I did; it was who I was. My identity was completely wrapped up in my rank, my aircraft, and my mission. But now, what was I?

Who was Ben Morley when he was not Lieutenant Colonel Morley? That question thrust me into what I now understand was an identity crisis. If you are reading this book, chances are you are in the middle of your own version of the same experience.

The Trap of Role-Based Identity

One of the biggest mistakes we make is confusing what we do with who we are. We tend to build our entire sense of self around our job title, our role, and our position within an organization or family system. We say, "I am a CEO," "I am a teacher," "I am a mother," or "I am a pilot."

But here's the problem with role-based identity: roles change. You can lose jobs, positions can be eliminated, companies can be sold, children grow up and leave home, and retirement eventually happens.

If your identity is heavily tied to your job, what happens when that role disappears? I learned this valuable lesson observing other military retirees.

Some successfully transitioned into civilian life, while others faced years, even decades, of struggle to find their footing. The key difference was not their qualifications or experience, but rather the foundation of their identity. When that shifted, they found themselves lost and unsure of their identity.

In contrast, those who thrived recognized that their military service was an action they performed, not the essence of who they were. Their core identity was built on values, character, and a sense of purpose that transcended any specific role. I've seen this same dynamic play out in the business world during my consulting work.

I've worked with executives who felt devastated when their companies were acquired and their positions eliminated. It wasn't just about the financial impact; they faced an identity crisis as they grappled with who they were without their title. I've encountered business owners preparing for M&A who became nearly paralyzed at the thought of selling their companies. It wasn't the money they feared; it was the inability to envision their identity separate from being "the founder" or "the owner."

In one particular case, a business was up for sale, and the buyer was eager to proceed. However, during a facility tour, the seller repeatedly pointed out issues with their own equipment, undermining the buyer's interest. At one point, the buyer had to ask, "Do you really want to sell the business?" The seller's answer was ultimately no, as he couldn't imagine his life without the business. Although his wife was ready to sell immediately, he couldn't envision who he would be without it, which led him to sabotage what seemed like a guaranteed sale.

This illustrates why succession planning is not solely about financials and operations; it's fundamentally about the transition of identity.

ACTION STEP: Audit Your Role-Based Identity

→ Write down the top three roles through which you currently define yourself (e.g., CEO, founder, parent, expert, leader).

→ For each role, ask honestly: *If this role disappeared tomorrow, what would remain of my sense of self?*

→ Ask the harder question: *Am I currently making decisions to protect my role or to serve the mission?* Like the business owner who sabotaged his sale, role-based identity can cost us far more than we realize.

→ Those who navigate transitions most successfully are the ones who can answer these questions clearly before the transition forces the answer.

The Construction Project

Most people don't realize that our identity is a construction project that begins the moment we are born. From childhood, we absorb countless messages about who we should be, what we should value, and how we should behave:

- Good boys don't cry.
- Smart kids get good grades.
- Successful people work hard.
- Leaders are confident.
- We should be grateful for what we have.

Layer by layer, we construct our identity based on these external influences.

We learn to emphasize the parts of ourselves that receive positive responses from others while hiding the aspects that do not elicit those responses. Over time, we develop a persona, or a social "mask," that we present to the world.

The issue arises when we begin to believe that this mask is our true identity. I grew up in a household that highly valued achievement. Good grades, athletic success, and leadership positions garnered attention and approval.

Consequently, I became very adept at achieving. I learned to set goals, work hard, overcome obstacles, and deliver results. This dedication earned me an appointment to the U.S. Air Force Academy, where I was also recruited to play football.

At the Academy, my skills thrived in an environment that rewarded achievement, discipline, and performance. However, I did not realize the consequences of this. I became so skilled at fulfilling the system's expectations that I lost touch with my true self beneath those accomplishments. It wasn't until I left the military that I began questioning what I genuinely cared about, what energized me, and what felt authentic rather than performative.

ACTION STEP: Examine Your Constructed Persona

→ Think back to the household or environment you grew up in. What behaviors, achievements, or qualities consistently received approval?

→ What parts of yourself did you learn to hide or suppress because they did not earn the same positive response? These are the messages that built your mask.

→ Now ask: *Which of those rules still govern my behavior today, even though they were written by someone else, for a world I no longer live in?*

The Loyalty Problem

A major obstacle to discovering our authentic identity is what I call "misplaced loyalty." We often remain loyal to outdated versions of ourselves long after they have ceased to serve us.

For instance, if you were the "responsible one" in your family, you might have learned to prioritize others' needs over your own. While this identity served a purpose when you were younger, it may now hinder you from setting healthy boundaries. If you were labeled the "smart one," you might have always felt pressured to have answers, making it difficult to admit when you need help. Similarly, if you were known as the "tough one," you may have learned to push through difficulties without showing vulnerability, which could prevent you from forming deep connections with others.

We remain loyal to these old identities even when they limit us because they feel familiar and safe. We know how to be that person, even if it doesn't help us reach the next level of life to which we are being called.

I spent years being loyal to "Achiever Ben," the version of myself that equated worth with external accomplishments. Even after leaving the military, I continued trying to prove my value through results, metrics, and recognition. However, I eventually realized that while that version of myself had served me well, it was actually holding me back from accessing my full potential.

The person I needed to become, someone who could help other leaders navigate complex transitions, required a different relationship with success, failure, and self-worth. I had to be willing to let go of the identity that had brought me this far in order to step into the one that could take me where I needed to go.

ACTION STEP: Identify Your Outdated Loyalties

→ What role or label were you given early in life—the responsible one, the smart one, the tough one, the peacemaker, the achiever?

→ Where has that identity served you? What did it make possible? What did it help you survive or accomplish?

→ What is it currently costing you? What do you avoid, suppress, or sacrifice in order to stay loyal to that old version of yourself?

→ Ask the defining question: *Is the version of me I'm protecting the one that got me here, or the one that will take me where I need to go?*

→ Letting go of an old identity is not betrayal. It is growth. The identity that carried you this far deserves your gratitude, not your permanent allegiance.

The Calling Confusion

Many people get stuck in this area. They believe they are called to a specific role rather than to express their authentic self through whatever roles they inhabit. For example, someone might say, "I'm called to be a pilot," or "I'm called to be a teacher," or "I'm called to be an entrepreneur." However, we are not ultimately called to a role.

Roles are merely vehicles. You might be called to serve others, and that calling can manifest in teaching for a season, then coaching, and later consulting. The calling remains constant; what changes is its expression.

I used to think I was called to be a pilot, but I eventually discovered that my true calling was to help people and organizations operate more effectively under pressure. For many years, that calling expressed itself through military aviation. Now, it manifests through executive coaching, operational consulting, public speaking, and helping business owners prepare for transitions.

The calling has always been there; the role was just one way of expressing it. This is why people can feel lost when their role changes, even if the change is positive. They mistakenly believe they have lost their calling when, in reality, they have only lost one expression of it.

Understanding this distinction is crucial for anyone going through a major transition. You are not starting from scratch or discovering something entirely new about yourself. Instead, you are uncovering what has always been within you and finding new ways to express it. That uncovering process requires the same disciplined curiosity I learned to apply in aviation and consulting—looking past the obvious for what's actually there. I call it "identity archaeology."

ACTION STEP: Separate Your Calling from Your Role

→ List the major roles you have held throughout your life, professionally and personally.

→ Look across all of them and ask: *What was I doing in each of these roles that felt most natural, most alive, most like me?*

→ Find the thread that runs through all of them. That thread is closer to your actual calling.

→ If your current role disappeared tomorrow, that thread would still be present. The question is not what role you would take next but how your calling would find its next expression.

The Archaeological Dig

Discovering your authentic identity is less about creating something new and more about uncovering who you have always been beneath the layers of conditioning, expectations, and role requirements. This process often begins with what I call "identity archaeology."

Examine the patterns in your life that have remained consistent, regardless of your roles or circumstances. Ask yourself: *What have you always been drawn to? What problems have you consistently noticed and wanted to solve? What types of people have you always been able to help? What activities make you lose track of time? What values have you never been willing to compromise, even when it costs you?*

For me, the archaeological dig revealed some interesting patterns. In every role I have ever held, from high school student body leader to military officer to business consultant, I have been drawn to operational excellence. I have noticed inefficiencies that others overlooked.

I find energy in the process of making systems work better. I have always been passionate about helping people perform at their best under pressure. Whether it was training pilots, leading teams through complex missions, or coaching executives through challenging decisions, that thread has been consistent throughout my entire adult life.

These were not skills I adopted for a role; they were ways of being that showed up regardless of my title.

ACTION STEP: Run Your Own Identity Archaeology

→ Consider these five excavation questions:

- *What have I always been naturally drawn to across every phase of my life?*
- *What problems do I consistently notice and feel compelled to solve, even when it's not my job?*
- *What activities cause me to lose track of time, regardless of whether I am being paid or recognized for them?*
- *What types of people have I always been able to help, and what is it about them that draws me in? What values have I never been willing to compromise, even when doing so would have been easier or more rewarded?*

→ Look for the patterns that appear across all five answers. What you find is not something new; it is something that has always been there, waiting to be named.

The Authenticity Test

How can you determine whether you are operating from your authentic self versus a constructed persona? There are some telltale signs. When you work from your authentic self, the work may be demanding, but it feels meaningful and energizing rather than solely draining. You have a natural energy for the tasks you engage in. You are not constantly trying to motivate yourself or push through resistance.

In contrast, when you operate from a persona, everything feels effortful. You find yourself trying hard to be someone you are not; you are performing rather than expressing. When you are authentic, you tend to attract the right opportunities and people more naturally. However, when performing, you may feel the need to work hard to convince others of your qualifications or worthiness.

Moreover, when you are authentic, you handle criticism and setbacks differently. They do not threaten your core sense of self because your identity is not dependent on external validation.

I remember the exact moment I realized I had found my authentic personal identity. I was working with a CEO who was preparing her company for acquisition. The operational improvements we implemented not only increased the company's valuation but also enhanced working conditions for employees and established better systems for sustainable growth.

At the end of the project, the CEO said something that stuck with me: "You did not just help us get ready for sale; you helped us become the company we have always known we could be."

That was when I realized my true calling: to help leaders and organizations become who they were meant to be. The specific methodology, whether Lean Six Sigma, operational excellence, executive coaching, or M&A preparation, is simply the vehicle I use.

ACTION STEP: Test Your Authenticity

→ Think about the work you did last week. For each major activity or interaction, answer honestly:

- *Did this feel natural and energizing or effortful and draining?*
- *Was I expressing who I am or performing who I think I need to be?*
- *Did I feel the need to convince others of my qualifications, or did the right people simply resonate with what I offered?*
- *When criticism or setbacks arose, did they threaten my sense of self, or could I process them without an identity crisis?*

→ A high number of "performing" answers is not a failure, but it is data. It tells you where the gap between your persona and your authentic self is currently the widest, and where the most growth is waiting.

The Integration Challenge

One of the biggest challenges in identity work is integration, or bringing together all the different aspects of who you are into a coherent whole. Most of us compartmentalize our lives; we have our work self, our family self, and our social self, each displaying different facets of our personality in different contexts.

To some extent, feeling like you have different versions of yourself is normal and healthy. However, if these different selves are so disconnected that you feel like you're living multiple lives, it indicates that you haven't integrated your identity around your authentic core. For me, integration meant weaving together my military strategic thinking, operational discipline, pressure-tested leadership, and an enduring desire to serve others.

Instead of viewing these as separate skill sets for different contexts, I began to see them as various facets of the same core identity: someone who helps leaders and organizations operate more effectively during times of pressure and transition. This integration allowed me to stop feeling like an imposter in business settings.

I wasn't trying to be someone I wasn't. I was simply being myself in a new context.

Permission to Evolve

Most of us are waiting for permission to be our true selves. We wait for our families to acknowledge we have outgrown old roles, for our colleagues to validate new directions, for our industry to accept our evolution, and for our community to approve our transformation.

However, the paradox is that the permission you seek can only come from you. No one else can give you permission to be authentic because no one else can fully understand who you are. They only see the versions of you they have encountered, which can often be quite limited. They may only know you as the person who fit their expectations, solved their problems, or played the role they needed you to play. They may resist your evolution because it threatens their understanding of where you fit in their world.

This is particularly challenging for high achievers who have been rewarded for fitting into systems and meeting external expectations. The very skills that contributed to your success, such as adaptability, performance, and meeting others' needs, can become obstacles to authentic self-expression.

I had to give myself permission to be someone other than the person the military had rewarded me for being. I learned to value things that weren't measured by traditional metrics and to care about outcomes that weren't always quantifiable.

This doesn't mean I had to reject everything about my previous identity. Rather, it involves choosing which aspects to retain and carry forward and which to let go of based on what supports my authentic expression, not what serves external systems.

The Business Identity

In my work with executives and business owners, I often see identity challenges manifest in specific ways. For instance, a founder may struggle to delegate because her identity is tied to being indispensable. A CEO might find it difficult to make tough decisions because her identity is built around being liked. An executive might resist adapting to changing market conditions due to their identity as an expert.

Business success frequently requires identity evolution. The skills and mindset that help you succeed at one level may not be the same ones you need to reach the next.

I once worked with a business owner who had built a successful company through personal relationships and hands-on involvement in every aspect of his business. However, as the company grew, his identity as "the guy who knows everything and does everything" became a limitation.

For the company to scale, he needed to transform, in his words, from "the doer" to "the developer," shifting from being an expert to an enabler. While the technical aspects of this transition were manageable, the real work was in changing his identity.

The Emergence Process

Authentic identity does not emerge all at once; it is a gradual process of experimenting with different expressions of who you are to discover what truly fits. This is why periods of transition can feel so uncomfortable.

You are not just changing what you do; you are discovering who you are. This discovery process requires experimentation, which means tolerating uncertainty and accepting occasional failure.

I spent the first two years after leaving the military exploring various professional identities, such as business consultant, executive coach, operational excellence expert, M&A advisor, and speaker.

Eventually, I realized that these were not separate identities but different expressions of the same core identity. I didn't have to choose just one; I could integrate them all under the umbrella of helping leaders and organizations navigate complex transitions effectively. However, I couldn't see this integration from the beginning. I had to explore each identity individually to understand how they all fit together.

ACTION STEP: Give Yourself Permission to Evolve

→ Identify the version of yourself that others currently expect you to be.

→ Ask honestly: *Am I maintaining this identity because it is authentically mine or because it is what others need from me?*

→ Name the next version of yourself that you sense is emerging. You don't need the full picture. What is one quality, value, or way of operating that belongs to that next version?

→ Identify one specific behavior or decision you have been postponing because it doesn't fit the current expectation. Take one step toward it this week.

→ Remember, you do not need your industry, your family, or your colleagues to grant you permission to become who you are. The permission they seem to withhold is the permission only you can give.

→ Transition discomfort is not a sign that something is wrong. It is the feeling of discovering who you are becoming.

The Fear Factor

One of the biggest obstacles to authentic identity expression is fear. This includes fear of rejection, failure, not being enough, and even being too much. What if the real you isn't as impressive as the persona you've been maintaining?

What if people don't like the authentic you as much as they liked your performative side? What if your interests and values don't align with what your industry or community expects? These fears are real and often stem from past experiences. Perhaps you faced criticism or rejection when you revealed your authentic self before. Maybe certain aspects of your identity were deemed unacceptable in your family, school, or early work environments.

However, I've learned that the fear of not being authentic is ultimately greater than the fear of being rejected for being authentic. When you are operating from a persona, you constantly feel anxious about being discovered. Conversely, when you are being authentic, you may encounter occasional rejection, but you are liberated from the exhausting effort of maintaining a false identity.

Surprisingly, authentic expression often attracts the right people and opportunities. When you stop trying to be everything to everyone, you become something specific to someone.

The clients I work best with are drawn to my unique combination of military background, operational expertise, and transition experience. I don't need to convince them of my qualifications; my authentic expression naturally attracts those who need exactly what I offer.

The Integration Journey

As we conclude this chapter on identity, I want to emphasize that identity integration is not a destination you reach and then leave behind. It is an ongoing process. As you grow, circumstances change, and you face new challenges, you will uncover new facets of who you are. The person you become in your fifties will be different from the person you were in your thirties.

This transformation does not mean you become someone else; rather, you reveal more of who you have always been. The goal is not to define your identity once and for all; instead, it is to develop the skill of authentic self-expression, enabling you to navigate future transitions and challenges from a grounded understanding of who you are.

Authentic identity doesn't arrive quietly. It walks directly into fear—fear of visibility, fear of failure, fear of being seen as who you really are rather than who you've convinced the world you are.

Learning to work with fear, not to eliminate it, but to navigate it, is essential for anyone wishing to live authentically in a world that often rewards conformity. The real question is not whether you will encounter fear as you embrace your authentic identity, but whether you will let fear stop you or teach you to access the courage you did not know you had.

REFLECTION: Who Would You Be Without the Mask?

→ Set aside fifteen minutes and answer the following questions:

- *Which fears have most shaped the identity I currently present to the world: fear of rejection, failure, not being enough, or being too much?*
- *What would I do, say, or pursue differently if I were certain the authentic version of me was enough?*
- *What aspect of my true self have I been concealing because I was not sure it would be accepted, and what has that concealment cost me?*

→ Name one specific area where you will choose authenticity over performance in the coming week. It does not need to be dramatic. It only needs to be real.

→ The goal is not to eliminate fear. It is to stop letting fear make your identity decisions for you.

→ What would you do if you knew that the people who matter most would not only accept the authentic you but had been waiting for that person to show up?

CHAPTER 4

Fear—The Guardian at the Gate

The email sat in my inbox for three days before I finally opened it. I knew what it was: an invitation to speak at a major industry conference.

Hundreds of senior executives from across the nation would be there; it was precisely the opportunity I had been working toward. So why was I terrified to even read it?

Sure enough, I was asked to deliver the keynote address titled "Leadership Under Pressure: Lessons from Military Aviation." It aligned with everything I had been building and was a chance to reach the exact audience I wanted to serve.

However, my first thought was not excitement or gratitude; it was pure terror. What if I wasn't as good as they believed I was? What if I froze on stage? What if someone in the audience knew more about military operations than I did and challenged me? What if I failed spectacularly in front of five hundred people, forever associating my name with that failure?

Fear had arrived right on schedule and was doing what fear always does: trying to keep me safe by keeping me small. But fear is the guardian at the gate. And the gate it guards is the entrance to my next level of impact and authenticity.

The Problem vs. Risk Distinction

Let me share something I learned in Air Force flight operations that completely changed how I think about fear and uncertainty. In aviation, we make a crucial distinction between problems and risks.

A problem is something that is occurring right now with 100 percent certainty and requires immediate action. A risk, on the other hand, is something that might happen, with an estimated probability and potential impact. Take a look at the following comparison:

- Problem → "We have insufficient fuel to complete this mission."
- Risk → "We may encounter weather that could force us to divert to an alternate airport."

Most of what we fear falls into the risk category, but our minds treat it like a problem. We respond to "I might fail at this presentation" in the same way we respond to "The building is on fire."

This is why fear can be so paralyzing. Our nervous system does not differentiate between actual danger and imagined danger. It floods us with stress hormones and triggers the fight-or-flight response as if the worst-case scenario is already happening.

During my years flying missions around the world, we constantly encountered genuine risks: weather that could affect the mission, threats from hostile forces, equipment malfunctions, and crew fatigue from crossing multiple time zones. We did not ignore these risks or pretend they did not exist, but we also did not treat them as problems that were already unfolding.

We assessed those risks, planned for them, and executed our missions while staying alert to changing conditions. The key was understanding what we could control and what we could only influence or monitor.

ACTION STEP: Classify Your Fears as Problems or Risks

→ Write down the top three things you are currently afraid of in your professional or personal life. For each fear, ask a single clarifying question: *Is this happening right now with certainty, or is this something that might happen?*

1. ______________________________

2. ______________________________

3. ______________________________

The Mindset Problem

I learned one of my most important lessons about fear during pilot training while watching a fellow student struggle to land the Northrop T-38 Talon. Nicknamed "the white rocket," the T-38 is a twin-engine supersonic trainer capable of rolling 720 degrees per second and reaching speeds of 820 miles per hour. It is among the most difficult aircraft in the Air Force to land.

My classmate had performed well in the T-37, the introductory jet trainer we flew in the first phase of training, but he was having trouble with the T-38, and his confidence was shattered. Defeat was written all over his face.

During one debrief, his instructor began with a question that surprised all of us: "So, how are you doing?"

The look on my friend's face seemed to ask, *Are you really asking me that? Is this a trick question?* No instructor had ever posed that question before.

The instructor continued, "I'm sensing feelings of defeat."

Immediately, the tension in my friend's body eased; someone finally understood how he was feeling. However, shame crossed his face, too.

"I don't think I'm progressing at the rate I need to," he admitted. "Maybe I don't belong here. I didn't have trouble landing the T-37, but I can't land the T-38."

The instructor's response changed everything: "The T-38 is one of the most challenging planes in the Air Force to land, and it takes time to become proficient. There is nothing in your grade book or in today's flight that makes me question your ability to learn this aircraft."

That was the turning point. My friend not only soloed in the T-38 but also earned his pilot wings and flew fighter jets. The issue was not his capability; it was his mindset. Fear convinced him that his current struggles indicated permanent inadequacy.

The Storyteller in Your Head

Fear can be considered a storyteller. It takes current circumstances and projects them into catastrophic futures. It uses limited information to construct elaborate narratives about why things will go wrong. The problem isn't that fear tells stories; it's that we believe those stories without questioning them.

Fear told my pilot training classmate, *You cannot land the T-38, which means you do not have what it takes to be a pilot, which means you do not belong here, which means you are going to fail out of training and disappoint everyone who believed in you.* Fear told me before my keynote speech, *You are going to get up there and forget what you want to say, or someone will ask a question you cannot answer, or they will realize you are not as qualified as they thought, and your entire consulting business will be destroyed.*

In both cases, none of that was true, but in the moment, it felt absolutely certain.

The key to working with fear is recognizing it as a storyteller, not a prophet. Fear can provide useful information about things to prepare for, but it is terrible at predicting actual outcomes.

ACTION STEP: Challenge the Story Fear Is Telling You

→ Write down the specific story fear is telling you about a situation you're avoiding or dreading. Then break it down into the chain of assumptions behind it: *This will happen which means that will happen which means everything will collapse.*

→ For each link in the chain, ask: *What is the actual evidence for this? Is there anything in my record (my actual history of decisions, results, and recovery) that truly supports this story?*

The Superpower Called Preparation

This brings me to one of the most powerful tools for transforming fear from paralysis into performance: preparation. This preparation needs to be strategic, addressing both the technical and mental aspects of what you are afraid of. Let me share a flight that taught me this unforgettable lesson.

I was flying for the first time in over three months after finishing my training in the Lockheed C-141 Starlifter when I noticed one of my oil gauges fluctuating erratically. It quickly became apparent that I needed to shut down the engine. I informed my crew, and immediately I heard concern in the voice of one of my crew members about flying with someone who had not flown in months and about handling one of the more threatening emergencies you can have, and there was little he could do to change the situation.

In contrast to his concern, I remained composed and self-assured, drawing upon countless hours of emergency training we had practiced as a crew. Familiar with the emergency procedure, we navigated the crisis confidently.

In such scenarios, fear and anxiety can easily take hold, making the situation seem dire, but preparation made all the difference. Flying any aircraft at any time involves inherent risks, much like operating a motor vehicle. What sets successful operators apart is not the absence of risk or fear, but rather their preparation. Preparation occurs on two critical levels: technical and mental.

Technical Preparedness

Technical preparedness involves anticipating potential challenges and formulating specific action plans for the most likely "what if" scenarios. While we cannot predict the exact circumstances, having a solid foundational plan for handling emergencies is invaluable when they arise. Preconceived actions enhance both reliability and accessibility.

When I received the invitation to present the keynote, fear immediately flooded my mind with thoughts of everything that could go wrong. Instead of allowing those fears to paralyze me, I used them as a checklist for preparation. Afraid that I might forget what to say? I prepared more thoroughly than ever before. Afraid that someone might ask a question I couldn't answer? I researched potential questions and prepared thoughtful responses. Worried that the audience might not connect with my military examples? I developed ways to translate my aviation experiences into business terms and prepared additional examples from my consulting work.

ACTION STEP: Build Your Technical Preparation Checklist

→ Identify an upcoming challenge, decision, or high-stakes event you are currently afraid of. Write down every fear you have about it, every "what if" your mind has generated. Now treat that list as your preparation agenda. For each fear, ask: *What specific action would reduce this risk or equip me to handle it if it occurred?*

Work through the three categories that appeared in the keynote example:

→ Performance fears (forgetting, freezing, stumbling): How can I rehearse until the material is in my bones, not just my notes?

→ Knowledge gaps (tough questions, being challenged): What do I need to research, and how will I handle gracefully what I genuinely don't know?

→ Connection gaps (audience not relating, examples not landing): What alternative approaches, translations, or examples have I prepared?

Mental Preparedness

Mental preparedness involves choosing in advance how you will emotionally respond to emergencies or challenges. By investing time and thought into this beforehand, you allow yourself to respond rather than react impulsively. Visualizing yourself in challenging situations while attaching positive feelings to them gives your brain a reference point, reducing the likelihood of panic. It demonstrates to yourself that you can remain calm in the face of adversity.

By the time I stepped onto that stage, I felt scared but prepared. Interestingly, my preparation didn't eliminate the fear; instead, it changed my relationship with it. Rather than viewing fear as a reason to back down, I learned to channel it into performance energy.

By combining technical and mental readiness, we equip ourselves to face uncertainty with resilience and confidence. This powerful approach benefits not just aviators but also those navigating life's unexpected twists and turns.

ACTION STEP: Build Your Mental Preparedness

→ Choose an upcoming high-stakes situation you are afraid of. Before it arrives, run through this mental preparation sequence:

- **Pre-decide your emotional response.** How do you want to feel and behave when the pressure arrives?
- **Visualize the challenge in full.** Close your eyes and walk through the scenario from beginning to end. Picture not just the ideal outcome but also the difficult moments, and picture yourself handling them with composure.
- **Attach a positive feeling to the picture.** What does it feel like to have navigated this well? Spend time in that feeling. Your brain cannot fully distinguish between the vividly imagined and the real.
- **Name the energy shift.** Preparation does not eliminate fear. Before the keynote, the fear was still present, but it became performance energy rather than a reason to retreat. What would it feel like for your fear to become fuel?

The Two Types of Fear

I have observed two types of fear in my work with executives and business owners during major transitions. The first type I refer to as a "danger fear." This is the fear of real threats to your well-being, like running out of money or damaging important relationships.

This type of fear often has a basis in reality and deserves attention. For example, if you are considering leaving a stable job to start a business, it's reasonable to be concerned about your financial security. Similarly, if you are implementing major changes in your organization, it is appropriate to worry about the impact on your team.

The key to addressing this fear of danger is to get specific. Ask yourself questions like, *What is my actual financial situation? How long could I manage with my current savings? What is my realistic timeline for generating revenue?* Most of the time, when you focus on the specifics of danger fear, you will find that the actual risks are more manageable than anxiety suggests.

The second type of fear is what I call a "growth fear." This refers to the fear of stepping into your full potential, of visibility, of success, and of being seen as who you really are rather than who you think you are supposed to be. This type of fear often disguises itself as practical concerns but mainly revolves around the ego. For instance, when someone asks themselves, *What if I am not qualified?*" it often means, *What if people see that I am not perfect?* Similarly, *What if it doesn't work?* really translates to, *What if I'm not as capable as I hope I am?*

Growth fears can be more challenging because they often feel like they're protecting you from failure, when in reality, they're protecting you from success.

The Imposter's Dilemma

Let me share an example involving Sarah, a client I worked with who was preparing her manufacturing company for acquisition. On paper, she appeared incredibly successful. She had grown the company from $2 million to $30 million in revenue in fifteen years. Her operational metrics were excellent, and her team was strong. Potential acquirers were very interested in her business. However, she was paralyzed by fear. She asked me during one of our coaching sessions, "What if they discover that I don't really know what I'm doing? What if they realize that I've just been making it up as I go along?"

To help her combat these feelings, I asked her to walk me through some of the major decisions she had made over the years. We discussed how she had navigated the 2008 financial crisis, managed major equipment failures that could have shut down production, and resolved conflicts between key employees that threatened to divide her management team. As she described her decision-making process in these situations, I pointed out something she could not see: "You keep saying to me you were 'just making it up,' but what you're really describing is sophisticated problem-solving under pressure. You gathered information, consulted with advisors, weighed options, made decisions, and adjusted based on the results. That is leadership."

Sarah's fear stemmed not from actual incompetence but from the gap between her internal feelings and her belief about how successful people are supposed to feel.

In reality, most successful leaders often feel like they are making it up as they go along. The difference is that they have learned to act despite that feeling, rather than allowing it to paralyze them.

ACTION STEP: Diagnose Your Fear Type and Apply the Right Response

→ Take a fear you are currently carrying and determine which type it is.

Is this DANGER FEAR?

→ If yes, get specific immediately and replace the anxiety with precise questions:

- What is my actual situation in numbers and facts?
- What is my realistic timeline and runway?
- What specific actions would meaningfully reduce this risk?

Is this GROWTH FEAR?

→ If yes, look beneath the practical-sounding concern to the identity question underneath it and walk yourself through your actual record of decisions made, problems solved, and crises navigated.

The Preparation Paradox

The more you prepare for something you are afraid of, the less intimidating it becomes. The paradox is that you cannot prepare perfectly for something you have never done before. This leads to what I refer to as the "preparation paradox." You need experience to build confidence, but you need confidence to gain experience.

The solution can be described as "progressive exposure." Instead of trying to eliminate fear before taking action, you take action in increasingly challenging situations while building your capabilities. In pilot training, our flight instructors did not wait until we felt completely confident before sending us off to fly solo. They built our skills gradually, first in the classroom and simulators, then with less instructor intervention, then in simpler aircraft, and finally, in more complex aircraft. Each step built our confidence for the next challenge.

I apply this same principle in my consulting work with executives to help them develop leadership skills. We do not start with the most challenging situations. Instead, we practice decision-making frameworks in lower-stakes environments first and build communication skills in safe settings before applying them to difficult conversations.

The goal is not to eliminate fear but to build the ability to function effectively in its presence.

The Perfectionism Trap

One common way fear disguises itself is through perfectionism. Beliefs like *I just need to be more prepared, I need to have all the answers,* or *I must eliminate any possibility of failure* often stem from perfectionism, which is not truly about excellence but rather about avoiding vulnerability. It's fear wearing a mask of productivity.

I once worked with an executive who had been preparing to launch a new product line for over a year. Each time we met, he seemed to have even more research to conduct, more data to analyze, and more scenarios to plan for. This endless preparation stemmed not from a lack of information, but rather from his fear of putting himself and his company in a position where they might fail publicly.

We needed to differentiate between productive preparation and fear-driven perfectionism. Productive preparation has a clear endpoint and focuses on the most likely scenarios. In contrast, fear-driven perfectionism is never-ending; it attempts to plan for every conceivable possibility.

The breakthrough came when he recognized that his competitors were not waiting for perfect information. While he was busy perfecting his analysis, others were gaining market share.

ACTION STEP: Distinguish Productive Preparation from Fear-Driven Perfectionism

→ Identify something you have been "preparing for" longer than a reasonable person would say is necessary. Run it through this diagnostic:

Productive preparation has a clear endpoint. It focuses on the most likely scenarios. It produces a plan you can execute. It gets you closer to action.

Fear-driven perfectionism has no clear endpoint. It keeps expanding to cover every conceivable scenario. It produces more research, never a decision. It keeps you further from action.

Then, ask the competitor question: *While I am perfecting my analysis, what are others doing? What am I allowing to happen by waiting?*

→ Apply the progressive exposure principle: You do not need to be fully confident before you begin. You need to take the next smallest step that builds toward the capability you're developing.

→ Perfect information will never arrive. The question is not whether conditions are ideal but whether you are ready enough to learn from what happens next.

The Courage Equation

Courage can be defined as action in the presence of fear. It is not the absence of fear; rather, it involves feeling fear and choosing to act regardless. This distinction is critical because many believe that they must feel brave before they can act courageously. However, it is quite the opposite. You build courage by taking action despite your fear, not by waiting for the fear to subside.

Each time you act while afraid, you prove to yourself that fear is not a reliable predictor of outcomes. You gather evidence that you can handle uncertainty, overcome challenges, and recover from setbacks.

I encourage executives and business owners to take what I call "courage-building actions." These are small steps that stretch their comfort zones without creating unmanageable risks. For example, it could involve having a difficult conversation they've been avoiding, implementing a much-needed operational change, or saying no to a client request that misaligns with their values. Each small act of courage makes the next one easier.

The Reframe Practice

Another powerful tool for addressing fear is learning to reframe the narratives it creates. Fear excels at generating compelling stories about why things will go wrong, but these narratives are often based on limited information and worst-case assumptions.

When fear warns, *This presentation will be a disaster,* you can reframe it as, *This presentation is an opportunity to provide value to those who need what I have to offer.* When fear asserts, *If this business decision fails, I'll lose everything,* you can reframe that as, *This decision involves risk, but I've prepared as well as I can. I will learn from whatever happens.* When fear tells you, *I do not know enough to take on this challenge,* you can reframe it as, *I have relevant experience and the ability to learn what I do not yet know.*

The goal is not to eliminate fear or pretend that everything will definitely work out. Instead, the goal is to achieve a more balanced perspective that considers both the risks fear highlights and the opportunities it overlooks.

ACTION STEP: Build Your Courage and Reframe Your Fear Narrative

The Courage-Building Action:

→ Name one action you have been avoiding because of fear, something that aligns with your values and goals but feels risky.

→ Make it smaller. What is the smallest version of that action you could take this week, one that stretches without breaking?

→ Commit to it publicly or in writing. Each act of courage, however small, builds the evidence base that fear is not a reliable predictor of your outcomes.

The Reframe Practice:

→ Write down the specific story fear is telling you about this situation. State it plainly.

→ Now rewrite it through a lens that acknowledges both the risk AND the opportunity:

- Ex: "This could go wrong in [specific way], AND this is an opportunity to [specific value I can provide / capability I can build / step I need to take]."

→ The goal is not to pretend everything will work out. It is to stop letting fear see only the risks while remaining blind to everything beyond the gate.

The Growth Edge

Fear often points toward your growth edge, the area where you are being called to expand beyond your current limitations. The things that scare you the most are often the very things you need to pursue for your development. This is not because struggle is inherently good, but because growth requires stepping outside your comfort zone.

When I reflect on the major transitions in my life, such as becoming the first student in my county to attend a military service academy, completing pilot training, transitioning from active duty to the reserves, moving from a military career to a civilian one, starting my consulting practice, and taking on larger speaking engagements, each of these experiences was preceded by significant fear. However, each time I moved through that fear rather than letting it stop me, I discovered capabilities I didn't know I had. I gained confidence that could only come from proving to myself that I could handle more than I initially thought.

That is why I tell my clients that fear can serve as a guidance system. When you feel afraid of something that aligns with your values and long-term goals, that fear may actually be pointing you toward your next growth opportunity.

The Transition Bridge

Fear is particularly intense during transitions because they require you to let go of the familiar before you can fully grasp the new. You are crossing a bridge between who you have been and who you are becoming, and the middle of that bridge can feel very uncertain.

In my work with business owners preparing for M&A transactions, I see this pattern repeatedly. They are not just selling a company but transitioning from one identity to another, from owner to former owner, from having ultimate control to trusting others with what they have built. The fear they experience is not merely about the details of the transaction; it is about the fundamental uncertainty of who they will be once it is over.

You cannot hold on to who you have been and become who you were meant to be at the same time. Fear has shown you where the grip is tightest. Now comes the harder work: learning to open your hands.

At some point, you must let go of the familiar to embrace the unknown. This process of letting go is where true transformation occurs.

REFLECTION: Let Fear Be Your Compass

→ Look at the fears that have been present in your life for the longest time—not fleeting worries, but the ones that have followed you through multiple seasons.

→ For each persistent fear, ask: Does this fear point toward something that aligns with my values and long-term goals or away from them? If it points toward your values and goals, that fear is not a warning to retreat. It is a signal that you are standing at your growth edge.

→ Name the bridge you are currently standing in the middle of. What familiar identity, role, or way of operating are you being asked to release? What is on the other side that you cannot yet fully see?

→ Complete this sentence in writing: "The fear I have been most reluctant to walk toward is ______, and if I am being honest, I think it is pointing me toward ______."

CHAPTER 5

Letting Go—The Art of Strategic Release

As I stood in my office at McChord Air Force Base for the last time, I looked at the walls where my certificates and awards had been displayed for years. All my years of military service condensed into a few boxes and a folder of paperwork.

The hardest part wasn't packing up my belongings, saying goodbye to my colleagues, or completing the final administrative tasks. The hardest part was letting go of who I had been. Lieutenant Colonel Morley was not just a title; it was my identity. It influenced how I thought about myself, how I made decisions, and how I navigated the world. This rank was not a label; it shaped every aspect of my life for nearly three decades.

However, I learned an important lesson about letting go: you cannot become who you are meant to be while holding on to who you have been. In every significant transition, you must release your grip on the familiar in order to reach for the unknown. This is a terrifying process because letting go always happens before you are certain that what you are reaching for will be there.

The Grip of the Known

Most of us underestimate how tightly we hold on to familiar patterns, even when they no longer serve us. We cling to old ways of thinking, outdated strategies, comfortable relationships, and familiar roles long after they have become limitations rather than assets.

Why do we do this? Because the known feels safe, even when it isn't truly serving us. The familiar is predictable, even when it limits our growth.

I often reflect on this in my work with business owners who are preparing to sell their companies. Intellectually, they want the transaction. They are eager for the financial outcomes, excited about new possibilities, and looking forward to the next chapter. Yet emotionally, they are terrified of relinquishing control. *What if the new owners do not understand the company culture I have established? What if they change systems that have worked well for years? What if they do not treat my employees the way I would?*

These concerns are valid, but beneath them lies a deeper fear: *Who will I be if I am not the owner of this company?*

Letting go involves more than just releasing external things; it requires us to release our internal attachments to identities, control, and the illusion that we can prevent uncertainty by tightly holding on to what we know.

ACTION STEP: Identify What You Are Clinging To

→ Name the role, identity, or situation you are currently holding most tightly. Be specific.

→ Ask the surface question: *What practical concerns am I using to justify staying in my current grip?*

→ Now ask the deeper question beneath those concerns: *Who will I be if I am not [this role, this title, this way of operating]?*

→ Recognize that your grip is not protecting you from uncertainty. It is creating the illusion that that's possible. Uncertainty is not caused by letting go. It is the condition that already exists.

→ Ask: *What is my grip on this currently costing me? In growth, in energy, in opportunity, in authenticity?*

Why We Stay Loyal to Stuckness

Sometimes we become loyal to our stuckness, even when we consciously desire change.

If you have never felt stuck at some point in your life, well, you probably have not truly lived. If you currently find yourself stuck in any way, there is no shame or embarrassment in that; it's simply a part of life.

Often, what we believe is keeping us stuck, such as a location, a job, or a relationship, is merely a symptom of a deeper issue. Beneath these recognizable problems, we can feel stuck emotionally, relationally, spiritually, or mentally. We often become trapped in systems that overpromise and underdeliver.

We often stay longer than we should, hoping for a breakthrough, a phone call, or a knock at the door, without realizing that another year has passed and we remain stuck.

A modern example of this shows up in the story of a mid-career professional I'll call Karen. For more than a decade, Karen worked at a large company that promised rapid advancement for "high potentials." Every year, she was told she was on track for a promotion "soon." Every year, she was given just enough recognition to keep her hopeful that the breakthrough was right around the corner. She stayed late, took on extra work, mentored junior colleagues, and waited for the moment when the system would finally reward her loyalty.

But the promotion never came. New organizational charts appeared, new leaders rotated through, and each time she heard a version of, "Stay patient, your time is coming."

When a friend finally asked her, "Do you actually want to build your future here, or are you just afraid to leave?" Karen realized she wasn't just an employee anymore. She was a captive of a system that ran on her hope and effort while giving her just enough in return to keep her from leaving. The company wasn't designed to help everyone rise; it was designed to keep as many capable people as possible in place, doing more than their share, for as long as possible.

Karen's situation is what I call a "career trap that thrives on stuckness." From the outside, it looks like a place you go to grow. From the inside, it quietly trains you to lower your expectations, rationalize delay, and normalize frustration. The system overpromises and underdelivers, but because everyone around you is playing the same game, telling the same stories about how things will eventually get better, it becomes hard to imagine anything different.

Like Karen, we can end up loyal to a system that is actually the main reason we remain stuck. We can create similar traps in our own lives: structures in our relationships, ways of thinking, and patterns of behavior that develop into multi-layered support systems for our stuckness. And stuckness tends to love company, doesn't it?

There are hidden benefits to remaining stuck that we often fail to acknowledge.

1. **Staying stuck avoids the discomfort and disruption that comes from being unstuck.** Change is challenging and can sometimes seem more daunting than we are willing to confront. Until the idea of getting unstuck becomes more appealing than remaining stuck, many of us will stay in place.

2. **Staying stuck shields us from uncomfortable emotions.** It is emotionally disruptive to take a chance on freedom. Breaking free from being stuck can evoke feelings of anger, resentment, fear, and unforgiveness, all emotions that are easier to avoid when we feel justified in our stuckness.

3. **Remaining stuck allows us to keep our story.** We get to maintain our narrative: *I'm stuck because of what they did to me. I'm stuck because of what happened.* If you choose to stay stuck, you can hold on to that narrative, which then becomes your new identity. The danger arises when you and your narrative become so intertwined that you lose the ability to see yourself without it. Who would you be without that story?

Consider an experienced manager named Luis who worked at a large company that went through a massive round of layoffs. Overnight, many of his closest colleagues and friends lost their jobs, while he remained employed. In the months that followed, the workload increased, the culture shifted, and the organization clearly wasn't the same place he had joined years earlier. On paper, Luis was "free" in ways his former colleagues were not, as he still had a paycheck, benefits, and options inside the company. But internally, he became trapped in a different kind of stuckness.

Luis started telling himself that he could no longer trust leadership. He stayed in the role, but mentally he lived in the past, rehearsing the unfairness of the layoffs and cataloging every new decision as further proof that the company was broken. Recruiters called with interesting opportunities, friends encouraged him to explore new paths, and he often caught himself daydreaming about doing work that felt meaningful again. Yet every time a possibility appeared, his internal dialogue pulled him back: *I put too much into this place to walk away now. They owe me. I shouldn't have to start over.*

In other words, Luis had been freed from one kind of external constraint but had adopted a victim mentality that kept him emotionally and professionally stuck. The company was no longer physically holding him there; his narrative was. He preferred the familiar misery of his current situation to the uncertainty of trying something new because, as frustrating as it was, it was at least predictable. Like many of us, he was choosing the dysfunction he knew over the freedom he didn't, clinging to an identity built around what had been done to him instead of who he could become next.

ACTION STEP: Audit Your Stuckness

→ Name honestly: Where in your life are you currently stuck? Professionally, relationally, creatively, or personally?

Ask whether you are in a system designed to keep you there (the Karen question):

→ Is this situation genuinely helping me grow or giving me just enough to keep me from leaving?

→ If I am being honest, am I building a future here, or am I afraid to leave?

Ask whether your own narrative is holding you in place (the Luis question):

→ Am I mentally living in a past event, replaying its unfairness and using it as evidence that things cannot change?

→ Is my story about what was done to me now more central to my identity than the story of who I am becoming?

Name the hidden payoffs you are receiving from staying stuck:

→ What discomfort am I avoiding?

→ What uncomfortable emotions am I not feeling?

→ What narrative am I protecting?

→ Who would I be without that story?

The Strategic Quitting Principle

This idea changed how I view the process of letting go. Are you familiar with the saying "Winners never quit"? I learned that winners actually quit all the time, but they do so strategically rather than reactively.

Many people perceive quitting as synonymous with failure, but strategic quitting focuses on resource allocation. It involves releasing good opportunities to make room for great ones. It's about letting go of what is merely okay in order to pursue what could be exceptionally rewarding.

The key difference between strategic quitting and reactive quitting lies in intention. Reactive quitting occurs when you feel frustrated or overwhelmed or try to avoid difficulty. On the other hand, strategic quitting occurs when you realize that continuing down a certain path, even if success is possible, would prevent you from pursuing something more aligned with your true goals.

During my final years in the Air Force, I was successful by every external measure. I had reached the rank of lieutenant colonel, leading important operations, and was well-respected by colleagues and superiors. I could have stayed for several more years and advanced further, but I began to understand that, while military success was meaningful, it no longer represented the best expression of my core calling. I was increasingly drawn to helping leaders in the civilian sector navigate complex operational challenges. I wanted to engage with business owners and executives focused on building rather than simply maintaining institutional systems.

Leaving the military was not an escape from failure but a step toward a fuller expression of who I was becoming.

ACTION STEP: Distinguish Strategic Quitting from Reactive Quitting

→ Identify something in your life you have been considering leaving, releasing, or stepping away from, and run it through the intention test.

Reactive quitting: *Am I considering this because I am frustrated, overwhelmed, or trying to avoid difficulty?* If yes, the urge to quit may be a signal to push through, not let go.

Strategic quitting: *Am I considering this because continuing, even if success is possible, would prevent me from pursuing something more aligned with my true goals and core calling?* If yes, this may be a strategic release worth making.

→ Ask the resource allocation question. Is this a good opportunity I am holding onto that is taking up space where a great one could exist?

→ Apply Ben's test. Was leaving a failure or a step toward a fuller expression of who I am becoming?

→ Strategic quitting is not giving up. It is directing your finite time, energy, and attention toward what matters most.

The Resourcefulness Revelation

One of the most significant obstacles to letting go is the belief that we need perfect resources before pursuing new directions. We often convince ourselves that we need more money, more experience, more connections, or more certainty before we can release our hold on our current situation.

I've learned that great teams and individuals excel at achieving a lot with limited resources. They prioritize resourcefulness over simply having resources. Allow me to share about a mission I flew that dramatically illustrates this lesson.

We encountered a cabin pressurization issue that could have become dangerous at altitude. Unfortunately, we didn't have access to the specialized repair equipment typically required to correct this problem. However, we did have some athletic towels and water from an onboard container. Using these basic materials and some creative problem-solving, we were able to resolve the pressurization leak and complete the mission safely. The solution did not come from having the perfect resources but from our resourcefulness. It was the ability to make the most of what was available.

This principle applies directly to both personal and professional transitions. You don't need to possess all the resources for your next chapter before letting go of the current one. Instead, you need to develop the confidence that you can be resourceful with whatever you encounter.

In my consulting work, I often see leaders who feel stuck because they wait for the perfect moment to make a change. They look for more savings, clearer market opportunities, or complete certainty about their next steps. However, perfect moments rarely arrive. What typically comes are imperfect moments that demand resourcefulness. The executives I work with who navigate major transitions successfully are not the ones who wait for ideal conditions. They are the ones who cultivate the ability to create value with whatever resources they have on hand.

The Apollo 13 Principle

One of my favorite examples of resourcefulness comes from the movie *Apollo 13*. When a catastrophic malfunction leaves the crew facing a deadly buildup of carbon dioxide, Gene Kranz in Mission Control doesn't ask, "What do you wish you had on board?" Instead, he challenges his team with, "What do we have on the spacecraft that's good?"

The astronauts ultimately survive by building a makeshift CO_2 scrubber from items already on board, showing that their lives depended less on ideal equipment and far more on their ability to use limited resources in innovative ways.

This is exactly the mindset required for letting go. Rather than focusing on what you will lose, concentrate on what you have available for the next phase of your journey.

When I left the military, I didn't have a business degree, extensive corporate experience, or a network of civilian executives. What I did possess was:

- Twenty-seven years of experience making decisions under pressure
- Deep knowledge of operational systems and process improvement
- Proven leadership ability to guide teams through complex challenges
- A strong understanding of risk management and crisis leadership

Instead of viewing my lack of traditional business credentials as a limitation, I chose to position my unique background as a differentiator.

The question is not whether you have everything you need for your next chapter. The real question is whether you can recognize the value in what you already possess and develop the resourcefulness to apply it in new ways.

ACTION STEP: Inventory What You Already Have

→ Write down everything you believe you are missing that is preventing you from letting go and moving forward. Be specific. Then, make a second list with every capability, experience, skill, perspective, and relationship you *already* possess.

→ For each item on your "what I'm missing" list, ask: *Is this truly required, or have I convinced myself it is required because it feels safer than beginning without it?*

→ Apply the differentiator lens: *What does my non-traditional background, unconventional path, or unique combination of experiences allow me to see or do that others in my next context cannot?*

→ Perfect resources will not arrive before the transition. Resourcefulness is the asset that carries you through it.

The Attachment Paradox

One of the most challenging aspects of letting go is what I term the "attachment paradox." Our greatest strengths can become significant limitations if we hold onto them too tightly.

The military taught me the importance of standard operating procedures, attention to detail, and adherence to established protocols. These were not just helpful habits; they were life-saving disciplines that ensured mission success and team safety.

When I transitioned to civilian business consulting, I initially tried to apply the same rigid adherence to established processes. I wanted detailed project plans with clear hierarchies and predetermined outcomes. I felt uncomfortable with the ambiguity and rapid adjustments that characterize much of business strategy work.

My attachment to military-style structure was not wrong; it had served me exceptionally well for several years. However, my inability to let go of that attachment when the context changed limited my effectiveness in this new environment.

The things we hold most tightly are often the ones we need to hold most lightly. Not because they are bad, but because rigid attachment to any one approach prevents us from adapting when circumstances change.

I've seen this pattern frequently with business owners preparing for acquisition. Their deep knowledge of their industry can become a limitation when they can't let go of "how things have always been done" to embrace new market realities. Their hands-on management style, which helped build the company, can become an obstacle when prospective buyers need to see systems that can operate without the founder's constant involvement.

The solution is not to reject your strengths; it is to view them as tools you can use flexibly rather than identities you must maintain rigidly.

ACTION STEP: Identify Your Strengths That Have Become Limitations

→ Name two or three strengths that have been central to your success so far. For each strength, ask: *In my current context or the one I am moving into, is this strength still an asset, or has it begun to function as a limitation?*

Signs that a strength has become a limitation:

→ You apply it automatically, regardless of whether the situation calls for it.

→ People around you have tried to give you feedback about it, and you have dismissed them.

→ It feels like part of who you are rather than something you choose to use.

→ You feel genuinely uncomfortable or threatened when asked to operate without it.

The goal is not to abandon what has made you effective. It is to hold your strengths with an open hand so they remain assets rather than anchors.

The Cocoon—The Space Between Who You Have Been and Who You Are Becoming

The most difficult part of letting go is what I call the "cocoon phase," a time when you have let go of the old but have not yet fully emerged as the new version of yourself.

Life has five seasons: winter, spring, summer, fall, and transition. We know how to navigate the defined seasons, but transition has no roadmap, no GPS to guide us through it. More people get lost in transition than in the harshest winter, because at least in winter, we recognize the season and know how to survive it.

Transition is like a hallway in your house, a space between rooms that is not meant for permanent living. We do not place our couches or TVs in hallways because they are transitional spaces, adjoining areas designed for movement, not for residence. When you're stuck in a transitional period, everything can feel squeezed, uncomfortable, unfamiliar, and inappropriate because you are not meant to remain there.

The Caterpillar Soup Reality

You already know what is happening inside that cocoon.

In the Introduction, I described a biological reality that most people have never encountered. The caterpillar doesn't simply grow wings. It dissolves. Everything, including its shape, form, function, and behavior, breaks down into a liquid state before anything new can be assembled. I called it "caterpillar soup." And I told you then that this was the central metaphor of the entire book.

Now you are living it.

This is the moment where that metaphor stops being a frame for understanding and becomes a description of your actual experience. The disorientation you feel in the middle of a major transition, the sense that what you were is no longer intact but what you are becoming isn't yet visible, is not confusion. It is dissolution. It is the cocoon doing exactly what it is designed to do.

During my own transition from military to civilian life, there was a six-month period when I felt completely liquefied. Like the caterpillar in the cocoon, the person I had been no longer existed, but the person I was becoming was not yet formed enough to be recognizable.

That period taught me that dissolution is not failure. It is the prerequisite. You cannot skip the soup and arrive at the butterfly. The only way through is through.

The Characteristics of the Cocoon

The cocoon phase is characterized by loneliness, isolation, fear, anger, and frustration. It can include disorientation, disruption, sleepless nights, and sometimes self-medication in various forms. It can include drinking, drugs, abusive behavior, and poor choices. If you recognize any of these behaviors in your own transition, be kind to yourself. This is part of the natural process of transformation.

The pain of transition lies in the awareness that something is happening inside you, but it has not yet named itself. You are letting go of what you know with one hand and reaching out in the dark with the other. Sometimes, while transitioning, you may not have anything in either hand for a while, and that can be terrifying.

What Survives the Dissolution

What I learned about the cocoon phase is that whatever is destined to travel with you through the transition will survive the dissolution and emerge with you transformed.

When you leave your cocoon, whatever is meant to be kept will stay with you, while whatever needs to be released will dissolve in the transformation process. This includes old identities, limiting beliefs, outdated security strategies, and relationships that were based on who you used to be rather than who you are becoming.

The cocoon phase is about letting go of your attachment to an old version of yourself because you finally believe that a better one is possible.

ACTION STEP: Recognize Where You Are in the Transformation

→ Ask yourself: *Am I currently in a cocoon? Have I let go of a previous version of myself without yet having arrived at the next one?*

→ If yes, name it specifically. What have I already released or lost, and what has not yet emerged to replace it?

→ Reframe the discomfort. If what you are feeling is loneliness, disorientation, frustration, or the sense that nothing in either hand is solid, that is not failure. That is caterpillar soup. It is the evidence that real transformation is occurring.

→ Do not try to rush back to the previous room or force your way into the next one. The hallway is uncomfortable precisely because you are not meant to live there, but you must pass through it.

→ Ask what you are afraid will not survive. Name the capabilities, values, and relationships you fear you are losing. These are your core, and they will emerge with you.

→ What needs to dissolve is not who you are. It is who you were required to be in a context that no longer fits.

The Dormancy Principle

It's important to understand that by letting go, you are not losing anything essential. You are not giving up parts of yourself that you will need later. Instead, you are releasing expressions that no longer serve your full potential. What appears to be lost is often just dormant, temporarily inactive, but not absent.

Dormancy is a muted presence. A volcano may be dormant, but it is not absent.

When I left my role as a military officer, it felt like I was losing my leadership identity, but I wasn't actually losing my ability to lead; I was simply releasing one expression of leadership to discover others.

The strategic thinking I developed in military planning evolved into business strategy consulting. The ability to perform well under pressure became a core part of my executive coaching approach. The systems thinking I used in operational roles transformed into process improvement consulting. Nothing essential was lost; everything was transformed.

This principle is crucial for anyone facing major transitions. The capabilities, insights, and strengths you have developed do not disappear when you change roles or contexts. Instead, they evolve into new expressions that may be even more powerful than the original forms.

The Timing Question

One of the most common questions I receive from clients is about timing: "When do I know it is time to let go?" There is no perfect formula, but there are usually signs that letting go is necessary for continued growth:

- **When your current situation feels too small for who you are becoming.**
  Like wearing clothes that no longer fit, staying in situations that were right for an earlier version of yourself can become restricting.

- **When you find yourself going through the motions without genuine engagement.**
  When work that once energized you starts to feel routine or meaningless, it may be time to consider what you want to emerge next.

- **If you're spending more energy maintaining the status quo than creating new value.**
  Sometimes we hold on to things not because they serve us, but because we have invested so much in them that letting go feels like admitting failure.

- **If you frequently come across opportunities that excite you but feel incompatible with your current situation.**
  Your authentic interests and emerging opportunities can signal directions you may want to take.

The key is learning to distinguish between temporary challenges that require persistence and fundamental misalignments that require change.

ACTION STEP: Know When It Is Time and Trust What You Will Carry Through

→ **Run the four timing signals against your current situation.**

- *Does my current situation feel too small for who I am becoming?*
- *Am I going through the motions without genuine engagement in work that once energized me?*
- *Am I spending more energy maintaining the status quo than I am creating new value?*
- *Am I regularly encountering opportunities that excite me but feel incompatible with where I am?*

→ If two or more of these are true, you may be facing a fundamental misalignment, not a temporary challenge that requires persistence. Now apply the Dormancy Principle to what you fear losing.

→ Name three capabilities or qualities that feel central to who you are. For each one, ask: How might this capability find a new and more powerful expression in the next chapter, rather than disappearing from it?

→ A volcano does not stop being a volcano when it goes dormant. And you do not stop being yourself when you let go of one expression of who you are.

The Business Application

In my work with companies preparing for M&A transactions, I often observe this challenge of letting go at an organizational level. Companies frequently struggle to release systems, processes, or even employees that were crucial for getting them to their current level but may not be optimal for their next phase of growth.

For instance, I worked with a manufacturing company that had built its success on the founder's personal relationships with key customers. However, as they prepared for acquisition, it became evident that this dependence on one individual's relationships was actually limiting their valuation. The company needed to move away from the founder-centric sales model and develop systems capable of functioning independently. This process wasn't about rejecting what had worked in the past; it was about evolving beyond those methods to create something more scalable and valuable.

Although the letting-go process was emotionally challenging for the founder, the outcome was a company that was not only more attractive to potential acquirers but also better positioned for sustained growth under new ownership.

The Trust Requirement

Ultimately, letting go requires trust. Not blind optimism, but a grounded confidence that you can handle whatever comes next, even if you cannot predict exactly what it will be. This trust is not about believing everything will work out precisely as you hope; rather, it's about having faith in your ability to respond effectively to whatever unfolds.

During my years flying international missions, we often encountered conditions that deviated from what we had been briefed to expect. Weather patterns would change, ground situations would evolve, and equipment would behave differently than anticipated. Our confidence did not stem from believing everything would go according to plan; it arose from knowing that we possessed the skills, experience, and resourcefulness to adapt to changing conditions.

The same principle applies to personal and professional transitions. You do not need certainty about outcomes; instead, you need confidence in your ability to navigate whatever outcomes may arise.

Understanding that you're in the cocoon phase, rather than feeling like you are failing at life, can completely transform how you approach the transition. The discomfort you feel is not evidence that you are moving in the wrong direction, but it signifies that real transformation is occurring. Just as the caterpillar must trust the process of dissolution to become a butterfly, you must trust that what feels like falling apart is actually essential preparation for becoming who you were meant to be.

The Practice of Release

Letting go is usually not a single dramatic moment; it is a practice, an ongoing series of small releases that gradually liberate you from old patterns and create space for new possibilities.

Perhaps this means saying no to requests that do not align with your values, even when saying yes might be easier. It could involve delegating responsibilities that you have always handled yourself or investing in learning opportunities outside your current area of expertise. Each small act of letting go builds your capacity for larger transitions when they become necessary or appealing.

In my own journey, learning to let go has been a continuous practice. I have let go of the need to have all the answers, the belief that my value comes from being indispensable, and old definitions of success that no longer reflect my authentic goals. This practice has been essential for navigating every major transition, both in my life and in helping my clients with theirs.

The Creative Space

Letting go creates space for creativity and innovation that were not possible when I was clinging to existing patterns. When you let go of the need to maintain old approaches, you open yourself up to discovering new solutions. By releasing predetermined outcomes, you become receptive to possibilities you had not previously considered.

Some of my best work with clients has emerged from this creative space. Solutions that neither the client nor I could have planned in advance often arise from the open-minded exploration that becomes possible when we are not rigidly attached to specific methods.

Letting go doesn't leave you empty. It leaves you available for something you could not have reached while both hands were full. What you choose to build in that space is what we turn to next.

REFLECTION: Begin Your Practice of Release

→ Letting go is not a single dramatic moment. It is a practice. This reflection is your first act of it.

→ At the organizational or professional level, what is one system, process, or way of operating that helped you reach your current level but may be limiting what comes next? What would it look like to evolve beyond it rather than simply defend it?

→ At the personal level, name one belief, definition of success, or need (e.g., to have all answers, to be indispensable, to be in control) you have been carrying that no longer reflects who you are becoming. What would change if you released it?

→ Recall a time when conditions deviated from what you expected, and you adapted effectively anyway. That experience is your evidence that trust is warranted. Write down what it taught you about your own resourcefulness.

→ What is one thing you can say no to, delegate, or step back from this week—not out of obligation, but because it no longer serves the person you are becoming?

CHAPTER 6

Redefinition—Becoming Who You Were Meant to Be

Ten months into my civilian career, I found myself sitting across from a potential client, a CEO whose manufacturing company was struggling with operational inefficiencies costing them hundreds of thousands of dollars annually.

"So, Ben," he said, leaning back in his chair, "tell me why I should hire a former Air Force pilot to solve my business problems."

Six months earlier, that question would have triggered my imposter syndrome. I would have fumbled through explanations about how military experience translates to business, apologized for not having an MBA, and tried to convince him of my qualifications despite my unconventional background.

But something had shifted within me. I had been through the work of awareness, resistance, identity, fear, and letting go. Now, I was ready for something new: consciously redefining myself not as someone trying to fit into established business-consultant categories, but as an individual bringing a unique combination of skills to address problems that traditional approaches often overlook.

"Here is what I see," I told him, pulling out a notepad. "You have a quality control issue that is manifesting as random defects in your production line. Your business consultants are treating this as a process problem, but I see it as a risk management problem. In aviation, we call this operational risk management, and we have developed systematic approaches for identifying, assessing, and mitigating risks before they escalate into failures."

For the next hour, we explored his operations using the risk assessment frameworks I had learned from years of flight planning. By the end of the meeting, we had not only identified the immediate problem but also uncovered the systemic vulnerabilities contributing to ongoing quality issues.

He hired me on the spot. Not despite my military background, but because of the unique perspective it offered.

Redefinition is not about becoming someone completely different. It is about consciously integrating who you have been with who you are becoming to create something new and authentic.

The Sigmoid Curve: Understanding the Science of Transitions

Before we delve further into the concept of redefinition, I want to introduce a powerful framework that explains why transitions can feel so disruptive and the importance of timing for major life changes.

Management thinker and social philosopher Charles Handy introduces the sigmoid growth curve in his book *The Age of Paradox.* This ubiquitous S-shaped curve not only illustrates the life cycle of any organization but also represents the life cycle of a product, any organism, the progress of a civilization, and even the course of a relationship.

Every new entity, whether a life, organization, project, initiative, or relationship, begins in a development phase, indicated by the bottom left starting point of the "S." It then enters the Introduction Stage, progresses to the Growth Stage, moves into the Maturity Stage, reaches the peak where it plateaus, and eventually declines and perishes.

If that were all there was to this concept, it would be quite discouraging. However, what makes it positive and encouraging is that an organization or individual can proactively start their own sigmoid curve at any stage they choose, rather than just watching the old curve rise over the hill, then decline, and eventually die out.

The Inevitable Dip

It's crucial to understand something about redefinition. During the Introduction Phase of any new growth curve, you almost always experience a dip, which can be seen as a setback. For individuals, this may manifest as a temporary but tangible drop in confidence, energy, effectiveness, and productivity.

Consider the parents of newborn babies. They know from experience that before an infant starts to grow after birth, it loses weight.

Similarly, when we encounter changes or embark on new initiatives during redefinition, we must recognize that when we locate ourselves in the Introduction Phase of a growth curve, a temporary dip is normal.

I personally experienced this during my transition from military to civilian life. In the first six months, I felt less competent, less confident, and less effective than I had in years. Each day felt like I was learning a new language while trying to solve complex problems. My energy levels were lower, my certainty was shaken, and I questioned whether I had made the right decision.

Understanding the sigmoid curve helped me realize that this dip was not evidence of failure. Instead, it was proof that I was in the natural Introduction Phase of a new growth curve.

ACTION STEP: Locate Yourself on Your Sigmoid Curve

→ Think about the major areas of your life and work (your career, a key relationship, your business, a leadership role) and where each lies on the sigmoid curve. If you are experiencing a dip right now in any area of your life, is that dip evidence of failure, or is it proof that you have entered the Introduction Phase of a new growth curve?

→ Name one area where reframing your current dip as a natural Introduction Phase would change how you are responding to it.

The Time of Great Confusion

Each new growth curve inevitably triggers what experts refer to as a "Time of Great Confusion." During redefinition, the old and new curves must coexist for a while. To manage the chaos, confusion, denial, and inevitable tension of sustaining both curves while preparing to let go of the older one, you need visionary entrepreneurial thinking and an optimistic, courageous mindset.

This period can be particularly disruptive for those who are invested in your old curve. Family, colleagues, and friends who are comfortable with who you have been may strongly resist your new direction and the changes it entails.

I witnessed this phenomenon firsthand as a pilot in the Air Force. The first jet I flew for eight years was being phased out and replaced by a new aircraft. There was substantial pushback from aircrew members who had devoted their entire careers to flying the older aircraft, and they directed their animosity at both the new jet and the personnel involved in its introduction. Some of these resistant crew members were so steadfastly opposed to adopting the necessary changes and training for the new jet that they chose to retire early instead. Although this new aircraft was superior to the old jet in almost every category, the reluctance to abandon the "old ways" became a constant source of tension.

A similar dynamic occurs during personal redefinition. Having support from others during your Time of Great Confusion can help you navigate these challenges. Think about your enthusiastic early January New Year's fitness resolutions, which often fade by the end of March. Introducing a new growth curve, such as getting in shape while still maintaining the old lifestyle, can cause chaos and confusion, especially if results are not yet visible. This is why having a support group, friends, and family to guide you through the dip is crucial as you strive to achieve the goals you set.

The Optimal Timing

The secret to sustained growth is to initiate a new growth curve before the old one peaks and begins to decline. The ideal point to launch a new curve is during the Maturity Phase of the existing one, which is to say the back side of the top of the "S," when it is on the upward slope toward its peak, not at the peak itself. Wait any longer, and the decline of the old curve will arrive before the new one has found its footing.

In today's rapidly changing world, some growth curves last only days or even minutes, rather than months or years. Successful individuals are those who recognize the signs of a mature curve and courageously initiate a new one at precisely the right moment.

When I decided to leave the military, I was not at the bottom of my career curve; in fact, I was near the top. I had achieved the rank of lieutenant colonel, was leading important missions, and could have continued advancing for several more years. However, I recognized that I was approaching the peak of the Maturity Phase of that particular growth curve, and if I wanted to successfully start a new one, I needed to act while I still had the energy, resources, and credibility from my military success.

Starting a new curve too early means you haven't fully maximized your current phase. Starting too late implies that you're attempting to launch from a position of decline rather than strength.

ACTION STEP: Manage the Time of Great Confusion and Choose Your Timing

→ If you are currently running two curves simultaneously (maintaining an old role, identity, or approach while building a new one), name both of them explicitly. Confusion often decreases simply by recognizing that you are in a time of great confusion, not a crisis.

Manage resistance from others. Who in your life is most invested in your old curve? How might their resistance show up, and how will you respond to it with clarity rather than defensiveness?

Build your support structure. Who is helping you through the dip? If you cannot name at least one person, that is your first action item.

Assess your timing honestly using the sigmoid curve:

→ Are you still in the Growth or Maturity Phase of your current curve—with time, resources, and credibility to launch from a position of strength? If yes, now is the window.

→ Are you already at or past the peak, maintaining rather than growing? If yes, you may be launching from a weakening position—act with urgency.

→ Are you too early, not yet having maximized your current phase? If yes, be deliberate about what you still need to extract from this curve before releasing it.

→ The ideal moment to begin your redefinition is not when circumstances force you to—it is while you still have the energy, resources, and credibility of a curve that has not yet peaked.

The Integration Opportunity

Many people approach career transitions or significant life changes as if they need to reject their past and start over from scratch. They believe that redefinition means abandoning everything they have been to become someone entirely new. But this isn't how authentic transformation occurs. Real redefinition is about integration, taking the best of who you have been and consciously combining it with who you are becoming, creating a new expression that is more aligned with your authentic nature.

When I left the military, I initially tried to downplay my aviation background, thinking I needed to become Businessperson Ben and leave Military Ben behind. I was attempting to fit into existing categories rather than creating a new category that honored all of who I was. The breakthrough came when I stopped trying to become someone I wasn't and began to embrace more of who I already was, expressed in a new context. The strategic thinking I developed through years of mission planning transformed into business strategy consulting. My ability to make decisions under pressure evolved into executive coaching for crisis leadership. My skills in systems optimization from military operations became operational excellence consulting, and the experience I gained training pilots translated into leadership development for business teams.

Nothing was lost; everything was transformed and integrated. Just as a butterfly emerges with capabilities the caterpillar never possessed, your redefined self integrates the best of who you have been with new capabilities you are now free to develop.

The butterfly does not reject its caterpillar past. Instead, it transforms that foundation into something capable of entirely new forms of contribution.

ACTION STEP: Map Your Integration

→ Draw a simple two-column table on a blank page. Title the left column "Who I Have Been" and the right column "How It Transforms."

→ In the left column, list the capabilities, experiences, disciplines, and ways of operating that defined your previous chapter, the ones you might be tempted to hide or downplay in your next context. For each item in the left column, ask: *How does this capability find a new and potentially more powerful expression in the next context I am moving into?*

→ Look for the transformation, not the abandonment. Mission planning becomes strategy. Decisions under pressure become crisis leadership coaching. Systems optimization becomes operational consulting.

→ Now ask: *What am I currently trying to hide or leave behind that might actually be my greatest differentiator in the next chapter?*

The Value Creation Shift

One of the most crucial aspects of redefinition is shifting from proving your worth to creating value. When you try to fit into existing categories, you expend immense energy proving that you belong, that you are qualified, and that you deserve to be there. Essentially, you are asking for permission to participate.

By redefining yourself based on the unique value you create, you stop seeking permission and start offering solutions to problems that need addressing. The butterfly does not attempt to convince anyone that it was once a caterpillar or apologize for its transformation; it simply presents what it can uniquely offer. It gains the ability to pollinate flowers the caterpillar could never reach and to see patterns from perspectives that are impossible at ground level. Similarly, when you stop trying to fit into existing categories and express your transformed capabilities, you do not need to justify your unconventional path. You simply demonstrate the unique value your particular combination of experiences allows you to create.

I see this pattern repeatedly in my consulting work. The most successful transitions occur when people stop trying to convince others they are qualified for existing roles and instead start creating new roles around their authentic capabilities.

For example, I worked with an executive who had spent twenty years in corporate finance but was passionate about sustainability. Instead of trying to convince environmental organizations that his finance background was relevant, he redefined himself as someone who helps purpose-driven companies build financially sustainable business models around environmental solutions. He did not abandon his financial expertise; he integrated it with his passion for the environment to create something new.

Within two years, he had built a consulting practice specifically focused on the intersection of finance and environmental issues, serving clients that neither traditional finance consultants nor environmental consultants could assist as effectively.

ACTION STEP: Stop Proving Your Worth and Start Creating Your Unique Value

→ Think about your current or most recent self-pitch. Are you primarily proving that your background is relevant to an existing category, or are you describing the unique value your specific combination creates?

→ Apply the permission test. Are you asking for permission to participate, or are you offering a solution to a problem that needs to be addressed?

→ Name the intersection. What is the specific combination of experiences, capabilities, and passions that only you bring, and what category of problems does that combination uniquely solve?

→ Complete this sentence: "I help [specific type of person or organization] who [specific problem they face] by [what you uniquely bring that others cannot]."

→ Notice the difference between the finance executive trying to convince environmental organizations that his background was relevant versus redefining himself as the person who helps purpose-driven companies build financially sustainable environmental solutions.

The Process Over Results Revolution

Let me share something that fundamentally changed how I approach both personal redefinition and client work: falling in love with the process rather than being obsessed with results.

Most people struggle with transitions because they fixate on specific outcomes. They want to know exactly what their career will look like, precisely how much money they will make, and, oftentimes, what their title will be. But here is the deeper problem: fixating on specific results often locks you into the person you already are. It limits you to outcomes your current identity can envision, rather than allowing the person you are becoming to discover what is actually possible.

Redefinition cannot be forced to a predetermined finish line. It unfolds through engagement, through the daily practice of developing new skills, serving others authentically, and creating value in ways that feel energizing rather than performative. When you trust that process, the results often exceed what your former self could have imagined.

I learned this by observing successful transitions across various fields. Those who reinvent themselves most fully are not the ones who locked onto the biggest goal and drove toward it. They are the ones who found ways to make the journey itself meaningful and allowed that meaning to reveal where they were headed.

If you are learning a new skill as part of your redefinition, seek methods that align with your learning style rather than forcing yourself through approaches that feel like drudgery. If podcasts during your commute work better than books, honor that. If hands-on experience teaches you more than classroom instruction, build your development around that reality.

The most sustainable process is the one that fits the person you genuinely are, not the one you think you should be.

The Walt and Roy Partnership

One of the most practical aspects of redefinition is understanding the difference between vision and execution, which I refer to as the "Walt Disney and Roy Disney dynamic." Walt Disney was the visionary, the dreamer who imagined possibilities that did not yet exist. Roy Disney, his older brother, was the planner, the behind-the-scenes implementer who figured out how to bring those visions to life. Walt himself acknowledged that, without Roy, he would have landed in jail several times for bouncing checks because of his disregard for financial realities. Roy kept Walt grounded and made their dreams financially viable.

Every successful redefinition requires both elements: a vision of what is possible and the practical planning needed to make it happen.

In my work with executives and business owners, I often observe a recurring issue on both sides of this dynamic. Some individuals are full of vision but lack a solid execution plan. They have inspiring dreams about their next chapter, yet no practical strategy for achieving those dreams. On the other hand, there are those who excel at planning but lack a compelling vision. They can create detailed project plans, yet lack the inspiring direction that makes their efforts meaningful.

The most successful transformations occur when you identify your own version of a "Walt-Roy partnership," either within yourself or by collaborating with others who complement your strengths. If you have a natural inclination towards being a visionary, partner with people who excel at implementation. Conversely, if you are more of an implementer, connect with individuals who can help you expand your vision of what is possible. Acknowledge that you likely possess a mixture of both capacities, but your natural tendency leans in one direction. As you develop, you can enhance your complementary skills instead of remaining dependent on others for what you lack.

If you see yourself as a Walt, who is your Roy? And if you identify more as a Roy, have you found your Walt yet?

ACTION STEP: Design Your Process and Find Your Partnership Balance

Design your sustainable process:

→ Identify one skill or capability central to your redefinition that you are currently developing.

→ Ask honestly: *Is the way I am developing this skill aligned with how I actually learn best, or am I forcing myself through an approach that feels like drudgery?*

→ Redesign your development approach around your natural learning style. The most sustainable process is the one you will actually sustain.

→ Name one daily or weekly practice that moves your redefinition forward in a way you genuinely find meaningful. Commit to it for thirty days before evaluating results.

Identify your Walt-Roy balance:

→ In your current redefinition, are you stronger as a visionary (Walt) or as an implementer (Roy)?

→ What evidence suggests you are leaning too far in one direction?

→ Name one specific person who complements your natural tendency. If you are a Walt, who is your Roy? If you are a Roy, have you found your Walt?

→ The most successful redefinitions combine a vision that pulls you forward and a process that makes daily progress possible.

The Hummingbird Approach

Another key principle for redefining yourself is what I call the "hummingbird approach." It emphasizes being curious and exploratory rather than fixed and rigid in your direction. A hummingbird moves from flower to flower, never lingering in one place for too long while gathering what it needs. In contrast, a woodpecker relentlessly hammers away at the same spot all day. Most career advice tends to encourage a woodpecker mentality: identify your passion and pursue it with unwavering focus.

However, I have found that curiosity often serves individuals better than a singular passion, particularly during phases of redefinition. Passion can make you feel as though curiosity is unnecessary once you believe you've found "your thing." Yet, curiosity keeps you open to possibilities you may not have previously considered. It allows you to uncover connections between various interests that can create unique value propositions.

When I left the military, I was curious about business strategy, organizational development, operational improvement, executive coaching, and speaking. I could have chosen to focus solely on one of these areas. Instead, I explored all of them and eventually discovered how to integrate them into a comprehensive approach to help leaders navigate complex transitions.

If I had been a woodpecker solely focused on operational consulting, I would have missed coaching opportunities. Similarly, if I had concentrated only on executive coaching, I would have overlooked the M&A advisory work. The hummingbird approach enabled me to discover the unique intersection of all my interests and capabilities.

ACTION STEP: Be the Hummingbird and Explore Before You Commit

→ List every area of work, learning, or service that genuinely interests or excites you right now, including ones that seem unrelated or impractical. Do not filter for practicality yet.

→ For the next sixty to ninety days, give yourself permission to explore at least three of these areas without committing to any one of them as "your thing."

→ As you explore, watch for the intersections, the places where two or more of your interests naturally connect and create something that neither could produce alone.

→ Ask the woodpecker test: *Am I narrowing my focus prematurely because I feel pressured to "pick something," or because I have genuinely discovered where my deepest value lies?*

The Myth of "Up and To The Right"

I want to address one of the most damaging myths surrounding redefinition and personal development: the belief that progress must always be linear, constantly moving "up and to the right" like a successful stock chart.

I think about a conversation I recently heard between two friends walking on a crisp Colorado fall day by the lake. It was their third lap around the water when Andrew finally asked the question weighing on him. "What should I do with my life?" This release of pent-up words brought him to tears. "I'm forty-four years old, and I have no idea if I'm doing the right thing."

His friend Jerry responded, "Andrew, no one knows if they are doing the right thing. No one! Whatever story you have been telling yourself about how you have failed, whatever 'should' you have been carrying about having it all figured out by now, is just nonsense, told to you by an outdated version of yourself."

This conversation captures something I see frequently in my work with executives and business owners. Variations of this story play out in countless settings: "Just give me the steps I need to follow to have the life I want." "How do I get customers?" "How do I convince people to hire me?" "How do I build a business?" "How do I raise money?"

These are all genuine, important questions, but they really serve as proxies for deeper existential inquiries: *Am I doing it right? Is it supposed to feel this confusing? Will I ever feel safe and successful? Where do I belong? What do I want from this life? Am I worth it? Have I earned my place?*

The Pressure of Constant Progress

Many of us want to know that we are making progress, that there is a clear path, and that we are on it. It's curious how desperate we can become to move up and to the right on the chart of life. We are convinced that only upward motion is part of the journey.

We live in a world that equates anything less than constant upward progress with failure. We are told that "up and to the right" is where happiness lives, where people never fear, never fail, and never struggle. Our economy thrives on the belief that where we are, down and to the left, is undesirable, and that if we just purchase the right solution, build the right company, or follow the right strategy, we will be safe and successful forever.

We tend to look at those who appear serene and accomplished, the embodiment of up and to the right, and fail to recognize the struggles they've endured. We project our desires and expectations onto them, wishing we could reach that point where everything is peaceful and we no longer face uncertainty.

Everyone else's journey seems easier. Their businesses appear more successful, and we often forget the hidden battles behind their accomplishments.

The Pathless Path

What if being lost is part of the path? What if we are meant to tack across the surface of the lake, sailing into the wind rather than wishing it was only at our backs? What if feeling lost, directionless, and uncertain about our progress indicates growth? What if it means you are precisely where you need to be on what I refer to as the "pathless path"?

Looking back at my own life, I cannot draw a straight line that moves up and to the right to define my journey, no matter how hard I try. None of it followed a linear progression that would conform to a traditional career planning chart.

The irony is that while the idea of moving up and to the right is appealing during times of struggle, it can also lead to isolation. If we were to achieve constant success, we might find ourselves utterly alone, disconnected from the very experiences that foster empathy, wisdom, and authentic connections with others.

The Comparison Trap

This pressure is heightened by the constant culture of comparison that surrounds us. Friends and colleagues, especially those building their careers, often become entangled in holding themselves to unrealistic standards, expecting a neat and straightforward unfolding of their lives. They compare their internal struggles, contradictions, confusion, and uncertainty against the polished success stories presented on LinkedIn and social media.

It is crucial to cut through the fog of useless and constant comparison, which can make us feel we are inadequate, broken, less than, and that we have come up short and are therefore unworthy of success. Social media portrayals of career success often distort and lie about the truth of professional development.

The path to a purpose-driven life can be messy, muddy, rock-strewn, and slippery. While we can try to play along with linear expectations, conforming without being true to ourselves can feel like slowly dying inside. This occurs when we quash our own truths and squeeze them to fit someone else's preconception of what it means to be a successful executive, entrepreneur, or leader deserving of respect and advancement.

The Courage to Embrace Non-Linear Growth

In moments of clarity, we must choose to leap across the chasm of false narratives that suggest our story is uniquely problematic or that our non-linear journey is evidence of failure to progress up and to the right.

Crossing this chasm of misconceptions can help us shed old identities and unlearn what confines, restricts, and entraps us. By achieving this clarity, we can discover who we truly are in the present, without the burden of defining who we will be in the future. This is the essence of authentic redefinition. It is not following someone else's prescribed path to success but creating our own based on our authentic nature and a growing understanding of where we can offer the most value.

The Integration Imperative

As Joseph Campbell observed, what we're ultimately seeking is not abstract meaning but an experience of being fully alive, a rapture of being alive. Building on this insight, we only touch that deeper aliveness when we are willing to integrate even the most shame-laden parts of ourselves, including our mistakes, missteps, and perceived failures.

This process means discovering who you are now by embracing your entire journey, not only the impressive highlights that look good on a résumé, but also the struggles, detours, and seasons of confusion and uncertainty. When we do this, we can release disappointments, missed goals, and the shame of not having everything figured out or living by someone else's timeline.

Aliveness in your career and leadership grows from integrating these diverse experiences and learning to forgive yourself for not following a straight-line path to success.

The Questions That Transform

This quest for clarity requires standing still, engaging in deep self-reflection, and learning to endure the discomfort of uncertainty. This new direction is about discovering your authentic purpose and tapping into that deeper sense of aliveness.

What would it feel like to let go of the need to know your ultimate plan? What if incremental progress, so long as it is directionally correct, were enough? What would it feel like to tack across the surface of that lake instead of racing straight to the other side as quickly as possible?

Whatever story you're telling yourself about your non-linear path is likely off the mark. Whatever is holding you back because your journey doesn't follow a straight-line trajectory is often outdated programming designed to keep you safe through conformity. The courage to embrace the unknown, to create white space for deep thought, and to seek clarity on who you are becoming rather than who you think you should be are all essential steps toward authentic redefinition. This process allows you to grow into the person you have always sensed within you, even if that person's journey looks nothing like anyone else's version of success.

REFLECTION: Embrace the Pathless Path

→ Write your honest answer to Andrew's question: "What have I been telling myself about how I have failed because my path has not been linear?"

→ Now ask Jerry's follow-up: "What if that story was told by an outdated version of myself, one programmed to stay safe through conformity?"

→ Map your actual path, the one that includes confusion, detours, and sideways movement alongside the growth. What has the nonlinear journey made possible that a straight line could not have?

→ Identify the comparison that is currently draining your energy the most. What polished version of someone else's journey are you measuring your internal experience against, and what are you conveniently leaving out about what their journey actually required?

→ Ask Campbell's question: What experiences, including your missteps, failures, and periods of confusion, have you not yet fully integrated into your story? What would it feel like to include them?

→ Complete this sentence: "The thing I most need to release my grip on in order to move forward as the person I am actually becoming is ______."

→ Your nonlinear path is not evidence of failure. It is evidence of a life being lived with genuine complexity, growth, and the courage to keep moving without a predetermined map.

The Authenticity Integration

True redefinition does not entail creating an entirely new persona. Instead, it is about allowing your authentic self to be expressed more fully than previous roles and circumstances allowed.

For most of my military career, many aspects of my personality and interests were dormant because they weren't relevant or valued in that context. My curiosity about business strategy, my interest in personal development, and my desire to work with entrepreneurs were always part of who I am, but they lacked outlets for expression.

Military culture rewards certain qualities, including discipline, hierarchy, mission focus, and team cohesion, while often suppressing others, such as individual creativity, questioning authority, entrepreneurial thinking, and emotional vulnerability. These qualities are not inherently wrong; military effectiveness requires certain constraints on individual expression for the sake of unit cohesion and mission success. However, this dynamic meant that parts of my authentic self remained underdeveloped.

Redefinition provided me the opportunity to integrate all aspects of who I am, not just those that were previously rewarded in my former context.

I did not have to reject the discipline, strategic thinking, and leadership skills I developed in the military. Instead, I could express them alongside the creativity, curiosity, and focus on individual development that had previously been dormant.

The Service Evolution

As you redefine yourself, one of the most important questions to ask is how you want to serve. Service often gives life meaning beyond personal achievement, but the ways you serve can and should evolve as you grow and as your circumstances change.

In the military, I served by defending national interests, training other pilots, and leading teams through complex operations. This service was clear and meaningful, but it was defined by institutional requirements rather than personal choice.

In my redefinition, I had the opportunity to choose how I wanted to serve based on my authentic values and my emerging understanding of where I could create the most value. I discovered that I wanted to help leaders navigate the transitions I had experienced myself. I aimed to assist organizations in optimizing their operations to produce better outcomes for all stakeholders. I wanted to help businesses prepare for successful transitions that honor what they have built while creating new possibilities. This was not a rejection of military service; rather, it was an evolution of my impulse to serve into forms that align more closely with my personal values and capabilities at this phase of my life.

The Practical Integration

Here are some practical frameworks for approaching your own redefinition:

1. **Skills Inventory:** Make a comprehensive list of the capabilities you have developed across all areas of your life, including professional, personal, volunteer, and hobbies. Look for patterns and connections between seemingly unrelated skills.

2. **Value Clarification:** Identify what you care about most deeply, not what you think you should care about. What problems do you notice that others may overlook? What solutions do you naturally gravitate toward?

3. **Energy Assessment:** Pay attention to which activities energize you versus those that drain you. Redefinition should move you toward more of what energizes you and away from what depletes you.

4. **Unique Intersection:** Look for the intersection between your skills, values, and energy, the place where you can create value by doing things that matter to you in sustainable ways.

5. **Market Reality:** Understand where your unique combination of capabilities can solve real problems for people who have the resources and motivation to address those issues.

The Continuous Evolution

It's crucial to understand that redefinition is not a one-time event. It is an ongoing process.

Redefining yourself is an ongoing process of consciously evolving as you grow, adapt to changing circumstances, and embrace new opportunities. The person you redefine yourself to be in your forties will differ from the redefinition that occurs in your fifties or sixties. This shift happens not because you are becoming someone entirely different, but because you are continuing to uncover and express more of who you have always been.

This perspective takes the pressure off the redefinition process. You don't have to get it perfect right away. You just need to take the next authentic step based on your current understanding of who you are becoming.

In my own journey, transitioning from a military officer to a business consultant was just the first iteration. As I've grown in confidence and capability, I've continued to refine and expand my professional identity to include speaking, writing, and various types of consulting work. Each iteration builds on the previous one while adding new dimensions that reflect ongoing growth and changing circumstances.

Understanding the sigmoid curve helps explain why this continuous evolution is both natural and necessary. Each redefinition represents a new growth curve, which will eventually reach its peak and require another thoughtful transition. The butterfly emerging from the cocoon isn't the end of its story; it's merely the beginning of a new chapter of growth and contribution. Similarly, each redefinition you undergo is not a final destination but rather a new platform for continued evolution and expanded service. Just as a butterfly's life cycle continues with migration, mating, and creating the next generation, your redefined self becomes a foundation for future growth, deeper service, and broader impact.

Creating Your Unique Category

Often, the biggest hurdle in redefinition is integration, or bringing together the various aspects of who you are into a coherent whole that resonates with both you and the people you serve.

This challenge is amplified if your background does not fit neatly into traditional categories. How do you integrate your military experience with business consulting? How do you combine technical expertise with leadership development? How do you merge analytical abilities with creative interests?

The key is to stop trying to fit into existing categories and to start creating new ones. Instead of asking, *How do I become a business consultant despite my military background?* consider asking, *How do I create a new type of consulting that leverages my military experience?* Rather than viewing your diverse interests as a liability, see them as a unique strength that allows you to serve clients in ways that specialists in any single area cannot.

Redefinition without action is just an interesting story you tell yourself. At some point, the new identity has to meet the world, albeit imperfectly, uncertainly, and sooner than feels comfortable. That moment is where the next chapter begins.

REFLECTION: Design Your Redefinition

→ Work through the five practical integration frameworks introduced in this chapter. Take thirty minutes and answer each in writing:

- Skills Inventory: List every capability you have developed across your entire life. Look especially for skills you take for granted because they come naturally. What patterns and unexpected connections do you notice?
- Value Clarification: What do you care about most deeply? What problems do you notice that others routinely overlook? What would you work on even if no one was watching?
- Energy Assessment: Which activities consistently energize you? Which consistently drains you? Are you currently moving toward more of what energizes you or defending more of what depletes you?
- Unique Intersection: Where do your skills, values, and energy all converge? That intersection, the place where you create value doing things that matter to you in sustainable ways, is the core of your new category.
- Market Reality: Who specifically has the problem your intersection solves, the resources to address it, and the motivation to act? How would you describe what you offer in one sentence?

→ Now ask the service evolution question. Based on what you have just discovered, how do you want to serve?

→ Redefinition is not a destination. It is the next authentic step. What is yours?

CHAPTER 7

Forward Motion—From Insight to Action

The phone call came on a Tuesday morning in September. It was from a CEO whose company was struggling with operational inefficiencies threatening a major acquisition. He had forty-eight hours to demonstrate that his organization could deliver consistent quality metrics, or the transaction would fall through.

"Ben," he said, "I know we've only talked once before, but I need help, and I need it now. Can you be here tomorrow morning?"

Six months earlier, I would have panicked. I would have spent hours researching the company, creating elaborate presentations, and trying to anticipate every possible question. I would have approached the situation as someone trying to prove they belonged in the room.

But something had shifted. I had done the internal work of awareness, worked through my resistance, clarified my identity, faced my fears, let go of old limitations, and redefined myself in line with my authentic capabilities.

Now I could respond from a place of grounded confidence. "I'll be there tomorrow at eight. Send me whatever operational data you have, and I'll come prepared with frameworks that can help us identify the real issues quickly."

When I walked into that room the next morning, I was not merely performing the role of a business consultant. I was being myself, someone who had spent decades optimizing complex operations under pressure and applying those skills to solve their immediate problem.

Within five hours, we identified the root cause of their quality issues, implemented interim solutions, and created a plan for sustainable improvement. The acquisition successfully moved forward.

More importantly for me, that experience crystallized something crucial about forward motion. Once you have done the internal work of transformation, taking action becomes natural rather than forced. You are no longer pushing yourself to do things that feel foreign to who you are; instead, you are expressing who you have become through aligned action.

The Goals vs. Plans Distinction

Before we discuss how to move forward effectively, we need to address a fundamental obstacle to taking action: the confusion between goals and plans.

The boxer Mike Tyson was being interviewed years ago about an upcoming fight. His opponent had been making statements to the press that he would knock out Tyson in the fifth round. When a reporter asked Tyson what he thought of his opponent's plan, Tyson famously said, "Everyone has a plan until they get punched in the face."

This quote serves as a perfect metaphor for how life often derails our carefully laid intentions.

The first mistake most people make regarding planning is confusing a goal with a plan. Saying, "I'm going to knock him out in round five," is a goal. It reflects a desire, a dream, or an ambition, but it is not a coherent plan.

To start, this opponent needs a strategy for rounds one through four. More importantly, he needs a plan for what happens if his idea fails to materialize and the fight goes beyond round five. What is his strategy for rounds six through twelve?

Once your initial idea is gone, after getting hit in the face in the first round, what will you do then? If your only plan is to reach round five without getting hit, especially against someone like Tyson, you don't have a plan; you have a fantasy.

This is a significant misunderstanding common among people trying to move forward. They often mistake enthusiasm, excitement, passion, and conviction for a real plan. These emotions can feel so strong that we convince ourselves we have a solid strategy when in reality we just have a goal.

Do not confuse a clear vision with a plan. While passion and desire are valuable and can help us persist in the face of resistance, they don't equip us with the skills and tools necessary for success.

When it comes to dreams and goals, far too much emphasis can be placed on visualizing Oz rather than designing and constructing the yellow brick road.

The U.S. Marines and Navy SEALs have a saying: "No plan survives first contact." In aviation, we often say, "The first thing to die in combat is your plan."

In the Air Force, I learned that having a plan that can be disrupted is different from having no plan at all. Every flight required multiple types of plans: flight plans, mission plans, and cargo and passenger plans. But what we actively engaged in before every flight was called "mission planning." We engaged in planning as a continuous process rather than a one-time event.

On longer missions, our aircrew's bags would fill with outdated mission plans along the way because of the dynamic nature of our operations. Many plans became outdated once we reached our destination, necessitating replacements before we could continue the mission.

I would tell my wife when I planned to return home from our mission, carefully using the word "planned." We never said "will" because plans can and did change frequently. The key to mission success was understanding that planning is an ongoing capability, not merely a static document. When circumstances changed, and they often did, we could adapt because we had developed the skill of planning rather than simply relying on its existence.

During the Crimean War in the 1850s, British officials knew their goal: to reduce deaths among wounded soldiers. But that goal alone wasn't a plan. When Florence Nightingale arrived at the military hospitals in Scutari, she found appalling sanitary conditions and extraordinarily high mortality rates from disease rather than battle wounds. Instead of relying on passion or vague intention, she built a multi-year plan grounded in data. She and her team collected detailed statistics on causes of death, living conditions, and hospital practices, then translated those numbers into visual "coxcomb" charts that even non-technical leaders could understand. Those visuals became her version of interpreting the goal, but what actually changed everything was the plan that followed: overhaul sanitation, redesign hospital layouts, improve ventilation and nutrition, and implement specific nursing protocols over time.

Her planning didn't stop when conditions changed; she treated planning as an ongoing capability, updating her approach as new data came in. The result was a dramatic reduction in mortality and, ultimately, a complete rethinking of hospital design and public health policy across the British Empire. Nightingale became influential not just because she cared deeply about wounded soldiers, but because she combined a compelling vision with a concrete, adaptive, multi-year plan.

Here is a framework for effective forward motion: have a goal, be clear, be inspired, and be enthusiastic, but recognize that having a goal alone is not enough. A goal is ephemeral, a wisp, a vapor. A plan is better than just a goal and is certainly necessary, but it can often become outdated. More importantly, you need to develop your capacity for planning and the ability to adapt when circumstances change. That is where the real value lies.

We are all going to get metaphorically punched in the face in some form, so have a plan that anticipates these setbacks and includes contingencies, as that is what great planning entails.

ACTION STEP: Build Your Planning Capability, Not Just a Plan

→ Think about a major goal you are currently pursuing in your work, your business, or your personal life. Write it down in a single sentence.

→ Now ask: *Do I have a plan, or do I just have a goal?* A goal tells you where you want to go. A plan describes the specific steps, sequence, and contingencies required to get there.

Assess your planning depth:

Do you know your first three concrete steps—not aspirations, but specific actions with owners and timelines?

Do you have a contingency for the most likely "punch in the face"—the obstacle or disruption most likely to derail you?

Is your plan a living document you revisit regularly, or a static intention you set and forgot?

→ Identify the single most likely disruption to your current plan. Write a brief contingency: "If X happens, I will Y." That one sentence transforms a goal into a real plan.

→ Remember: The goal of planning is not to produce a perfect plan. It is to develop your capacity to think, adapt, and act when conditions change.

The Critical Question: What Does Finished Look Like?

Even with sound planning, one more crucial element can make or break forward motion: clarity about what completion actually entails.

Let me share a disaster that illustrates what happens when "finished" is not clearly defined from the beginning. In the late 1620s, Sweden's King Gustav II Adolf set out to build a flagship that would dominate the Baltic Sea and advertise his growing power. He commissioned the Dutch master shipwright Henrik Hybertsson to design a large, heavily armed warship that would become known as Vasa.

From the outset, the king wanted not only firepower but also grandeur: the ship would carry two full gun decks with 64 bronze cannons and be covered with more than 700 carved and brightly painted sculptures proclaiming his glory and Sweden's ambitions.

As construction progressed, the project came under intense pressure. The king was frequently away at war but sent letters pushing for more guns and faster completion. The design was modified while the ship was already under construction, making her higher and more heavily loaded in the upper works than originally planned. Communication between the king, the admiralty, and the builders was poor, and no one had final, clear responsibility for balancing the ship's stability against the political demand for size, armament, and ornament.

Vasa was launched and rigged in Stockholm in 1628. A simple stability test—sailors running back and forth across the deck—had to be stopped after only a few passes because the ship heeled so alarmingly, yet no one with authority dared delay the maiden voyage.

On 10 August, with officials and crowds watching, Vasa set out with her lower gunports open to fire a ceremonial salute. A modest gust of wind struck her sails, the ship heeled, water poured in through the open gunports, and within about 15–20 minutes, she had sunk in Stockholm harbor, less than a mile from where she cast off. Around 30–50 people died, and one of the most expensive warships Sweden had ever built lay on the bottom—undone not by the enemy, but by unclear requirements, political pressure, and constantly redefining what "finished" looked like.

This disaster illustrates a critical principle for effective project management. You must clearly define what completion looks like before you begin and then protect that definition against scope creep. For some projects, this may be easy to determine, while for others, it may prove more challenging.

There should always be clearly defined start and finish lines. For instance, if a process is currently operating at 25 percent efficiency but the goal is to achieve 30 percent, then 30 percent would be the definition of "done" for that project. While it sounds simple, remember that even the King of Sweden struggled with this fundamental requirement.

It can be easy to overlook, especially when a project is already underway. If you have ever watched a home improvement show where the homeowners are involved, you may have noticed a recurring pattern. Often, the project exceeds its budget, extends its timelines, or both. While it's sometimes unavoidable, other times it's because homeowners continually change their definition of what a finished project looks like. They may want to add new features or remove certain elements, forcing designers to adjust their plans on the fly to satisfy the homeowners. In these situations, homeowners fail to adhere to their initial definition of project completion.

The answer is to define your project's scope from the start and stick to it. By clarifying which departments, activities, or outcomes are included in each phase, you can ensure that all other elements are considered out of scope. This exercise aims to prevent scope creep, as tragically exemplified by the story of the Vasa.

If your supervisor, partner, or even you yourself becomes the "creeper," shifting the goals and definitions of completion while the project is underway, it is essential to politely but firmly defend the original scope. Remember, the scope of the project has already been determined and agreed upon. Perhaps those new suggestions could form the basis for a different project in the future.

This principle extends beyond professional projects. For instance, if you're planning to clean the garage, do you know what your end goal looks like? Do you have sufficient time to accomplish the entire task right now? Or can you break the project down into manageable parts and clearly identify what you want to achieve at each milestone?

By defining what "finished" means to you and scoping the project appropriately, you can significantly increase your chances of success in all of your endeavors.

ACTION STEP: Define Finished Before You Begin

→ Think of a project, initiative, or goal you are currently working on or one you are about to start. It might be a business initiative, a personal development goal, a home improvement project, or a team deliverable.

→ Answer these three questions in writing:

What does "finished" look like? Describe the specific, observable outcome that marks completion. Not "improve customer satisfaction," but "customer satisfaction scores reach eighty-five by Q3."

What is explicitly out of scope? Name at least two things that might naturally creep in but are NOT part of this project. Writing them down makes them easier to defend against later.

Who has the authority to change the scope, and what is the process for doing so? Scope creep is most dangerous when it happens informally. Build in a deliberate review gate.

→ If you are already mid-project and the scope has drifted, stop. Explicitly renegotiate the definition of "finished" with all stakeholders before continuing. The Vasa sank because no one was willing to have that conversation.

The Start with Zero Principle

I want to share a transformative meeting that changed my approach to problem-solving and taking authentic action.

Mike Evangelist (yes, that's his real name) was working on DVD-authoring software around the turn of the millennium, when creating DVDs was still a complex, professional task. The systems were expensive, aimed at experts, and came with thick manuals full of technical detail. After Apple acquired the technology his team had been working on, Mike joined Apple and was asked to help shape a consumer DVD-burning application that would eventually become iDVD.

Inside Apple, Mike and his colleagues did what they'd always done: they tried to take a complex, professional-grade workflow and make it more approachable. They sketched features, thought through options, and prepared to explain their ideas to Steve Jobs. By the time the meeting came, they had invested real effort in thinking through the problem and felt proud of the work they were about to show.

When the meeting began, Jobs didn't spend time on their slides or detailed explanations. Instead, he walked to a whiteboard and drew a simple rectangle. "This is the application," he said. "It has one window. You drag your video into the window. Then you click the button that says 'Burn.' That's it." There would be no pop-up dialogs, no complicated sequences of steps, and no visible complexity for the user to manage.

That, in essence, is what Apple built.

For Mike, the moment was jarring. All the nuance and technical sophistication he and his team had prepared seemed to vanish in a few strokes of a marker. But over time, he came to see the power of what Jobs had done. Instead of starting with a complicated system and trying to simplify it, Jobs started from zero and asked what the simplest possible experience should be—and then insisted that everything else serve that vision.

Starting from zero means determining the minimum number of steps required to achieve your goal, regardless of how others perceive it. This process is not about taking someone else's approach and merely scaling it down; it's about starting from scratch and building only what is essential. You aren't trying to improve an existing process; you are discovering what completion actually requires.

What you want is completion. If you don't complete the task, then it isn't done. By starting from zero and working forward, you can evaluate each proposed step to determine if it truly needs to be there. If it does, you can further assess whether there are any wasteful activities within that step that can be streamlined.

By starting with zero, you act as a gatekeeper from the inside out, protecting against unnecessary complexity instead of attempting to tackle a complex system from the outside in. The traditional approach may yield some improvements, but beginning from zero can lead to transformational results.

This is precisely what I teach my consulting clients. Many have identified multi-million dollar savings or streamlined processes from weeks to days. Others have reduced project times from hours to just five minutes.

In my own work, I apply this principle consistently. When a client presents me with their operational challenges, I don't start by fixing their existing systems. Instead, I begin with zero and ask, "What outcome are you actually trying to achieve? What is the minimum number of steps required to get there reliably?"

Sometimes, the answer bears no resemblance to the current approach. Sometimes, it reveals that we are solving the wrong problem entirely. But starting with zero always leads to more authentic and effective solutions than trying to improve an existing complex system.

Consider where you can apply this philosophy of starting from zero, either personally or professionally. Instead of asking, *How can I improve this?* ask, *If I were starting from nothing, what would I actually need to accomplish this goal?*

ACTION STEP: Start With Zero on Your Most Complex Process

→ Identify one process, workflow, or routine in your work or life that feels unnecessarily complicated, something where the number of steps, approvals, or moving parts seems out of proportion to the actual result you're trying to achieve. Do not try to improve it yet. Instead, set it aside entirely and answer this question from scratch: ***What is the single outcome I actually need from this process?*** **Then ask:** ***What is the absolute minimum number of steps required to reliably achieve that outcome?***

Build that minimum process on paper. Do not look at the current process while you do this.

→ Now compare your zero-based process to the current one. Every step in the current process that does not appear in your zero-based version is a candidate for elimination or consolidation.

→ Apply this same question to a personal decision you are overthinking: "If I were starting from nothing, what would I actually need to make this work?" The answer is often simpler and more actionable than anything you could derive from the current tangle.

The Collaboration vs. Consensus Distinction

One of the biggest obstacles to forward motion is the belief that everyone needs to agree on the direction before moving forward. I've learned that there is a crucial difference between collaboration and consensus.

Consensus means that everyone must agree before any action can occur. In consensus-driven cultures, people spend enormous amounts of time trying to ensure everyone is on board with every decision. This often leads to slow progress, risk aversion, and mediocre outcomes.

Collaboration means working effectively with others towards a common goal, even when not everyone agrees on every detail. It means making timely decisions with input from relevant stakeholders and then moving forward with commitment, even if the decision wasn't unanimous.

Seth Godin has a great saying: "Nothing is what happens when everyone has to agree."

In my work with leadership teams, I see organizations get stuck in endless rounds of discussion when they should be moving into action. They confuse talking about change with actually implementing it.

The leaders who create real forward motion understand that it is easier to educate a doer than to activate a thinker. They would rather work with people who are committed to action and can learn along the way than with those who want to analyze everything perfectly before moving forward.

This does not mean making reckless decisions without input. It involves gathering appropriate information, considering relevant perspectives, making the best decision possible with the available data, and then committing to that direction while remaining open to course correction based on results.

REFLECTION: Collaboration or Consensus?

→ Think of a decision or initiative in your work or life that has been stalled, one where forward motion has been slow, unclear, or absent. Is the delay due to a genuine need for more information, or is it a consensus trap?

→ Ask yourself:

Who actually needs to be consulted before this decision is made?

Who needs to be informed of the decision after it is made?

Who simply wants to agree before anything moves, and is that requirement serving the goal or protecting someone's comfort?

→ Identify one decision you have been waiting to make until everyone agrees. Commit to making it, with the right input, but without requiring universal consent, within the next forty-eight hours.

→ Remember, collaboration produces better decisions. Consensus produces delayed ones.

The Three Horse Rule for Innovation

Let me share an idea that revolutionized my approach to generating solutions and moving forward: The Three Horse Rule.

In creative brainstorming, there are three types of ideas, each represented by a different horse.

Thoroughbred Ideas are reliable and have been used before. They represent the safer, more conservative solutions with a proven track record of producing results. They are the go-to approaches when predictable outcomes are needed.

Mustang Ideas are wild but can be tamed. While they are untested and require more effort to implement, they possess significant potential. These ideas stretch beyond the familiar, yet are not entirely outlandish.

Unicorn Ideas are imaginative, ridiculous, and even unreasonable. They are the kind of suggestions that prompt people to ask, "Why would you even think of that?" However, unicorn ideas often lead to breakthrough innovations.

Most organizations and individuals tend to stick with thoroughbred thinking, relying on familiar approaches because they feel safe and predictable. The problem is that thoroughbred thinking only yields thoroughbred results.

If you want breakthrough outcomes, you must be willing to explore Mustang and Unicorn possibilities.

For instance, Apple, Tesla, Uber, and Amazon were all born from Unicorn Ideas. These were not logical extensions of existing approaches. They were innovations that defied logic and were acted upon with courage.

In my consulting work, I always encourage clients to generate all three types of solutions before deciding which direction to pursue. The Thoroughbreds offer a reliable fallback. The Mustangs present opportunities for significant improvement. The Unicorns open up possibilities that were previously unconsidered.

Typically, the best forward motion comes from combining elements from all three categories, using Thoroughbred methods to implement Mustang goals with Unicorn creativity.

ACTION STEP: Run All Three Horses

→ Choose a real challenge you are currently facing, be it a business problem, a career decision, a leadership dilemma, or a creative block. Write it at the top of a page.

→ Now generate three solutions, one from each category:

Thoroughbred: The reliable, proven approach. What has worked in situations like this before? What would the conventional expert recommend?

Mustang: The bolder, untested approach. What would you try if you weren't worried about it not working? What would require some courage but might produce significantly better results?

Unicorn: The unreasonable, imaginative approach. What would you do if there were no constraints? Let it be ridiculous.

→ Now look across all three. Is there a combination that you haven't yet considered?

→ The goal is not to implement the Unicorn. The goal is to let the Unicorn loosen your thinking enough to see possibilities the Thoroughbred alone would never reveal.

The Hell Yeah! Or No Filter

One powerful tool I've learned for maintaining momentum is what Derek Sivers calls the "Hell Yeah! or No" filter.

The principle is straightforward. If you're not exclaiming "Hell Yeah!" about an opportunity, then your answer should be no. If you don't feel anything like "Wow, that would be amazing! Absolutely!" then you should decline.

While this mindset may seem extreme, it is rooted in an important insight. Saying "yes" to mediocre opportunities prevents you from being available for exceptional ones. Many successful people reach a point where the issue is not a lack of opportunities but being overwhelmed by "kinda cool" commitments that bury them alive and render them B-players, despite having A-player skills.

The author Tim Ferriss writes about the following philosophy in his work: "To develop your edge initially, you learn to set priorities; to maintain your edge, you need to defend against the priorities of others."

Early in your career or business, you may need to say yes to various experiments to discover what you're best at and what you're passionate about. However, once you achieve a reasonable level of success, it becomes essential to be more selective.

I learned this lesson the hard way during my first two years as a consultant. During that time, I said yes to nearly every opportunity out of fear of turning down potential business. I worked with clients who weren't ideal fits, took on projects that didn't align with my strengths, and spread myself too thin by juggling too many different types of work.

The result was mediocre outcomes for clients and burnout for me. I was busy, but I wasn't building the focused expertise and reputation that would attract the clients I truly wanted to serve. Everything changed when I started applying the "Hell Yeah! or No" filter.

I began declining opportunities that were merely "good" to make room for those that were "great." As a result, I worked with fewer clients but produced much better outcomes. My reputation improved, my energy increased, and my income actually went up despite doing less work.

REFLECTION: Apply the Hell Yeah! or No Filter

→ Look at your current calendar and commitments. Write down every significant obligation, project, or opportunity on your plate right now.

→ Apply the filter honestly to each one. Mark it:

Hell yeah!—This genuinely excites me. I would choose it again today.

Kinda Cool—I'm doing this out of obligation, habit, or fear of missing out, not genuine enthusiasm.

No—I should never have said yes to this, and I know it.

→ For everything in the "Kinda Cool" column: What would it take to exit, delegate, or complete it quickly so it is no longer occupying space on your calendar and in your mental bandwidth?

→ For the next thirty days, practice saying "I'll think about it" instead of an automatic yes, then apply the filter before you respond. Note how it changes the quality of what you commit to.

→ The goal is not to be busy. The goal is to be effective, and effectiveness requires protecting your bandwidth for work that is genuinely aligned with who you are becoming.

The Process vs. Results Revolution

In Chapter 6, we explored how falling in love with the process — rather than fixating on results — unlocks identity. In this chapter, that same principle becomes the engine of sustained action. Here, it is not about identity; it is about discipline.

Most people struggle to take consistent action because they focus too much on outcomes they cannot directly control. They want to know exactly how much money they will earn, when they will reach their goals, and what recognition they will receive before they are willing to commit to the work. The problem is that this orientation has it backwards. Focusing primarily on results often prevents you from taking the consistent actions that actually generate them.

When you fall in love with the process, such as daily practices, skill development, and value creation activities, the results tend to take care of themselves, often exceeding your initial projections.

I frequently see this pattern in my work with executives and business owners. The individuals who achieve the most success are not necessarily the ones who set the biggest goals; they are the ones who establish sustainable practices around activities that create real value and then show up to those practices regardless of whether results are yet visible.

This is what separates forward motion from wishful thinking. If you are building a consulting practice, fall in love with the process of understanding client challenges and developing solutions. If you are growing a business, fall in love with the process of creating value for customers and optimizing operations. If you are developing your leadership, fall in love with the process of learning from every interaction and applying those insights immediately.

The specific outcomes become less urgent when you are genuinely committed to the process that produces them. That commitment is what keeps you in motion when results are slow, and it is what compounds over time into results that outpace anything you could have planned for at the start.

The Strategic Starting Framework

One of the biggest obstacles to forward motion is the belief that you need to know everything before you can start anything. People often wait for perfect information, complete certainty, and ideal conditions, which seldom materialize.

However, I have learned that you discover who you are and what you're capable of by doing the work, not just by thinking about it. Austin Kleon discusses this in terms of "fake it till you make it," but not in a deceptive way.

He means to pretend to be creating something until you actually do. Practice being the person you want to become until that practice becomes your natural expression. If you aspire to be a business strategist, start doing business strategy work, even if it's for free, even if it's for small organizations, and even if you feel underqualified, take action.

If you want to be a speaker, start speaking at local organizations, community groups, or industry meetups. Don't wait until you feel ready to present at major conferences. If you aim to be a consultant, begin consulting for people in your network in areas where you have some expertise on problems you genuinely want to help solve.

The experience will teach you things you can't learn through preparation alone. You will discover what you are naturally good at, what energizes you, the types of clients you work best with, and which approaches create the most value.

This does not mean being irresponsible or claiming expertise that you do not possess. It means being transparent about your experience level while offering whatever value you can at your current capability.

ACTION STEP: Start Before You Are Ready

→ Identify one role, capability, or aspiration you have been waiting to pursue until you feel more ready, more qualified, or more certain. Write it down.

→ Now identify the smallest possible version of that thing you could do this week.

If you want to be a speaker, identify one local group, association, or company team meeting where you could present a fifteen-minute talk.

If you want to be a consultant, identify one person in your network with a problem you know how to solve and offer to help, for free if needed.

If you want to be a writer, publish one piece of writing this week.

→ The goal of this first action is not to be impressive. It is to break the inertia of waiting. You cannot refine something that doesn't exist yet.

→ You are not faking expertise you don't have. You are practicing being the person you are becoming with full transparency about where you are on that journey.

The Momentum Principle

Forward motion creates momentum, making subsequent actions easier. Conversely, lack of action leads to stagnation, making any action feel difficult.

This is why the first step is often the hardest, regardless of how small it is. Once you are in motion, maintaining it requires much less energy than starting from a complete stop. In physics, this is described as the difference between static friction and kinetic friction. It takes more force to get an object moving than to keep it moving once it has started.

The same principle applies to personal and professional development. It takes more energy to begin a new practice than to sustain it once it is established. It requires more courage to have the first difficult conversation than the tenth. It takes more effort to create the first piece of content than the hundredth.

This is why I encourage clients to focus on getting started rather than striving for perfection. The goal of the first iteration is not to create a masterpiece but to overcome the inertia of not moving. Once you are in motion, you can refine, improve, and optimize. But you cannot refine something that doesn't exist yet.

The Feedback Integration System

Sustainable forward motion requires a feedback system that allows you to course-correct based on actual results rather than theoretical projections.

Many people either avoid feedback entirely because it may indicate they are not performing as well as they hoped or feel overwhelmed by it, making it hard to process effectively. The key is to integrate feedback into your normal process rather than treating it as a separate and threatening activity.

In aviation, we debrief after every flight. The goal was not to criticize performance but to extract valuable lessons that would improve future flights.

We examined what went well so we could replicate it, what didn't go as planned so we could avoid it, and what new insights emerged so we could apply them moving forward.

I employed the same framework in my business development approach:

- **What's Working?** What activities are delivering the most value to clients? Which methods feel most natural and energizing? Which results are exceeding expectations?

- **What's Not Working?** What activities are consuming energy without delivering proportional value? Which approaches feel forced or inauthentic? Which results are falling short of expectations?

- **What Am I Learning?** What insights are revealing my strengths, ideal clients, and most effective methods? What patterns am I noticing that suggest new directions or approaches?

This regular integration of feedback prevents small issues from escalating into major problems and helps identify opportunities for improvement before they become obvious.

ACTION STEP: Build Your Weekly Debrief Practice

→ Set aside twenty minutes at the end of each week, or after every significant project, meeting, or client engagement, and answer these three questions in writing:

What's Working? What activities delivered the most value? Which approaches felt natural and energizing? What results exceeded expectations?

What's Not Working? What consumes energy without proportional results? What felt forced or inauthentic? What fell short of expectations?

What Am I Learning? What patterns are emerging? What do this week's results reveal about your strengths, your ideal clients, or your most effective methods?

→ The goal is navigation. Aviation crews debrief every flight not to assign blame, but to fly better next time. Treat your weekly review the same way.

→ After four weeks of consistent debriefs, look across all four. What single change, one thing to do more of or one thing to stop, is most clearly indicated by the pattern you see?

The Compound Effect

One of the most powerful aspects of consistent forward motion is the compound effect. Small, consistent actions that may seem insignificant on their own can create dramatic results over time.

Most people tend to overestimate what they can accomplish in a short period and underestimate what they can achieve over a longer duration through consistent effort. The executives I work with who achieve sustainable success are not the ones who make dramatic changes overnight. Instead, they make small, consistent improvements that accumulate over months and years.

For instance, a business owner who improves operational efficiency by two percent every quarter does not see immediate, dramatic changes. However, over three years, those small improvements compound into a 25 percent increase in efficiency, significantly affecting profitability and company valuation.

Similarly, an executive who dedicates thirty minutes daily to strategic thinking will not transform their leadership overnight, but over time, this consistent practice develops strategic judgment, giving them a competitive edge.

The key to leveraging the compound effect is choosing actions that are:

- **Sustainable:** Actions you can maintain consistently without burning out.
- **Cumulative:** Each iteration builds on the previous ones.
- **Aligned:** They guide you toward your authentic goals.

The Integration Challenge

As we conclude this chapter on forward motion, I want to address one of the greatest challenges: integrating authentic action with practical constraints.

You have done the internal work. You understand who you are, what you want to create, and how you want to serve. However, you also have real-world responsibilities, financial obligations, and practical limitations that cannot be ignored.

The solution isn't to choose between authenticity and practicality; it's to find ways to move in authentic directions while respecting these practical realities. Perhaps you cannot immediately transition to your ideal role, but you can start developing relevant capabilities. Maybe you cannot launch your own business right away, but you can begin building the relationships and expertise you will need. You might not be able to relocate to your preferred location immediately, but you can start creating the financial foundation that will make it possible.

The goal is consistent movement in authentic directions, not immediate arrival at ideal destinations. Forward motion does not require perfect conditions; it requires clear direction and consistent action aligned with who you are becoming, rather than being limited by who you have been.

You can move forward with great discipline and still be performing a version of yourself that was designed for someone else's approval. Forward motion earns its full power only when the person moving is actually you. That is the work that remains.

REFLECTION: Your Forward Motion Inventory

→ Take stock of where you are right now. Work through each of the frameworks in this chapter and identify the one that is most directly relevant to where you are stuck or where you have the most forward motion available.

Goals vs. Plans: Do you have a goal or a genuine plan with contingencies?

What Does Finished Look Like: Is your definition of completion clear and agreed upon, or are you building the Vasa?

Start With Zero: Is there a process, decision, or approach you need to redesign from scratch rather than improve?

Collaboration vs. Consensus: Is something stalled because you are waiting for agreement that will never come?

The Three Horse Rule: Have you been riding only Thoroughbreds when a Mustang or Unicorn solution might be what's needed?

Hell Yeah! or No: Is your calendar filled with obligations that are consuming bandwidth you need for work that genuinely matters?

→ Choose the one framework where honest application would create the most movement. Commit to one specific action in the next seventy-two hours.

→ Forward motion does not require perfect conditions. It requires clarity about direction and the willingness to take one aligned step now.

CHAPTER 8

Authenticity—The Courage to Be Yourself

I was sitting in the conference room of a Fortune 500 company, surrounded by executives in expensive suits, discussing a multi-million-dollar operational improvement initiative. The conversation had been going in circles for forty minutes, filled with sophisticated business jargon, complex frameworks, and impressive-sounding strategies that failed to address the real issue at hand.

Finally, I did something that would have terrified me six months earlier. I stopped trying to sound like everyone else in the room.

"Can I share what I'm seeing here?" I said, pulling out a simple notepad. "You are treating this as a business process problem, but it's actually a crew resource management issue. In aviation, when multiple people with good intentions work at cross purposes, we don't need better procedures; we need better communication protocols."

The room fell silent. I could sense them processing whether this military guy was about to waste their time with irrelevant analogies. However, I proceeded to explain exactly how aircrew coordination principles could resolve their operational dysfunction. I drew simple diagrams on the whiteboard and used straightforward language that was clear rather than impressive. I shared real examples from my military experience instead of hiding behind business school terminology.

By the end of the meeting, we had identified solutions that their previous consultants had entirely missed. More importantly, I discovered something crucial: authenticity is not just more fulfilling than performance; it is more effective. When you stop trying to be what you think others want and start being who you truly are, you can provide value no one else can because no one else has your unique combination of experience, perspective, and capabilities.

The Marble and Dust Principle

Before we delve deeper into the concept of authenticity, I want to share something that revolutionized how I think about self-perception and confidence.

Each of us has the power to decide what leaves a lasting impact on our lives. Pain and failure are just as significant as victories and joys, yet we often choose to emphasize the former over the latter. Great leaders acknowledge setbacks, struggles, and trauma without letting these experiences define them. They choose to record these challenges in dust rather than stone, refusing to tattoo themselves with markers of regret, failure, and suffering. Instead, they etch their victories and successes in marble.

Why do they do this? Because they understand the importance of remembering significant positive events, especially during tough times. When individuals are governed by their emotions, they allow the shame of their failures and setbacks to infiltrate their mindset.

When we write down our negative emotions in dust and start commemorating our successes in stone, we learn which elements of our lives contribute positively to our growth. We begin to value ourselves more highly and teach others to respect us in the same way. The highs and lows of our journeys are valid, but we have a terrible tendency to dismiss our successes as fleeting and eradicable, while treating our failures as permanent scars that we must carry.

We have the power to decide that nothing in life should scar us. Our setbacks should not bring us shame but offer valuable lessons, while our victories deserve to be celebrated and remembered as important milestones.

We must stop allowing our strengths to be erased and blown away by the oppressive momentum of shame and unworthiness. We must allow our injuries to be overshadowed by what matters far more to us in the grand scheme of things.

This principle transformed how I approached my transition from military to civilian life. Instead of focusing on what I was losing or what I lacked compared to traditional business consultants, I learned to write these concerns in dust and carve my unique strengths and experiences in marble. Over the course of twenty-seven years, I developed strategic thinking, crisis leadership, and operational excellence, which were not deficits to overcome. They were assets etched in stone that no one could take away or replicate.

REFLECTION: Record Your Marble and Dust

→ Take a blank page and draw a line down the middle. Label the left column "Dust" and the right column "Marble."

→ In the Dust column, write the setbacks, failures, and struggles you have been allowing to define you—the things you have been treating as permanent scars. Name them plainly, without minimizing or dramatizing them.

→ In the Marble column, write the victories, capabilities, and experiences that belong etched in stone—things you have been dismissing as ordinary or erasing from your self-narrative entirely.

Now ask yourself honestly:

Which column is longer, and which one do you spend more time reading?

What would change about how you introduce yourself, pitch your value, or show up in a room if you led from the Marble column instead of the Dust column?

→ Name one specific capability or experience you have been writing in dust that belongs in marble. Make it concrete—not "I have leadership experience" but the specific thing you did, under specific pressure, that no one else in that room could have done.

→ That is the version of yourself this chapter is asking you to lead from.

The Authenticity Deficit Disorder

Let me introduce you to what I call "Authenticity Deficit Disorder," or the condition that affects leaders who have been playing prescribed roles for so long that they forget how to be themselves.

These individuals become so adept at fulfilling the expectations of their organization, industry, or family that they lose touch with their authentic selves. They transform into "stuffed shirts," people who are thoroughly convinced of their own importance but have forgotten how to be human.

Throughout my military career, I frequently witnessed this phenomenon. Officers who had been "playing leader" for so long forgot that true leadership is about connecting with people, not merely managing systems. They became obsessed with processes, procedures, and protocols, losing sight of the human element that truly makes organizations function.

The higher you rise in any hierarchy, the more pressure there is to be inauthentic. You are expected to have all the answers, never show uncertainty, always project confidence, and maintain an image of complete control.

However, authentic leadership requires exactly the opposite qualities. It involves admitting when you don't know something, showing vulnerability when appropriate, asking for help when needed, and being willing to be wrong when new information emerges. The most effective leaders I have worked with, both in military and civilian contexts, are those who have learned to be genuinely themselves while fulfilling their responsibilities. They do not pretend to be perfect, but they are reliable. They do not claim to have all the answers, but they are committed to finding solutions. They do not try to impress people, but they consistently create value.

ACTION STEP: Diagnose Your Authenticity Deficit

→ Think about the role you occupy most consistently. Then answer these questions in writing:

What behaviors or expressions do you suppress in this role that feel genuinely like you?

When was the last time you admitted uncertainty or asked for help in a professional setting, and what stopped you from doing it more recently?

If a trusted colleague described the version of you they see at work, and a close friend described the version they know personally, how different would those two descriptions be? What accounts for the gap?

→ Identify one specific behavior you perform for the role that you would stop performing if the role were removed. That behavior is the leading indicator of your authenticity deficit.

→ This is not an indictment. Every leader has one. The leaders who build lasting organizations are simply the ones who notice it and consistently choose to close the gap.

The Confidence Paradox

Here is something counterintuitive that I discovered about authentic confidence: The more you try to appear confident, the less confident you actually become.

Real confidence is not about projecting an image of having everything figured out; it is about being comfortable with not knowing everything while trusting your ability to figure things out as you go.

For years, I believed confidence meant having the right answer immediately, speaking with authority on every topic, and never showing uncertainty. This approach worked very well in military culture, where decisive leadership under pressure was valued and rewarded.

However, in business consulting, this approach backfired. Clients did not want someone who pretended to know their industry better than they did. They wanted someone who could ask the right questions, listen carefully to their challenges, and apply relevant experience to their specific situation.

The breakthrough came when I stopped trying to impress people with what I knew and instead focused on connecting with them through my genuine curiosity. Rather than presenting myself as the expert who had all the answers, I became the experienced guide who could help them discover their own solutions.

This authentic approach to confidence proved more impressive to clients, as it demonstrated real expertise, the kind that comes from experience, not just knowledge. It showed that I was secure enough in my abilities to admit when I needed to learn something new.

The Publicly Support, Privately Critique Principle

One of the most challenging aspects of authentic leadership is learning to balance honesty with loyalty. It's crucial to be genuine while also supporting your organization and team.

I call this the "publicly support, privately critique" principle. In other words, be a public endorser of what your team is doing, while saving criticism and concerns for private conversations within appropriate forums. This approach is not about being two-faced or dishonest; instead, it's about recognizing that authenticity involves wisdom regarding timing, context, and audience.

Being part of a team gives you insider knowledge about challenges, limitations, and areas needing improvement. The public does not require that level of detail, nor should they have it. Your role is to represent your team's efforts positively while addressing legitimate concerns internally.

However, this principle only works when there are genuine opportunities for private critique. If leadership is resistant to feedback, if concerns are consistently dismissed, or if there is no real forum for honest discussion, then the principle breaks down. The only time I believe this guidance does not apply is when your private criticism is being ignored, and you feel the situation is genuinely harmful to those who cannot protect themselves.

During my final years in the military, I encountered leadership that was not receptive to feedback and seemed more focused on image management than actual problem-solving. That is when authenticity required me to step away rather than continue endorsing something I could not genuinely support.

REFLECTION: Locate Your Confidence Trap and Test the Publicly Support, Privately Critique Principle

→ On the confidence paradox: Think of a recent situation where you performed confidence rather than expressed it—where you spoke with more certainty than you actually had, deflected a question rather than admitted you didn't know, or positioned yourself as the expert when curiosity would have served better.

What were you afraid would happen if you had simply said, "I don't know the answer to that, but here is how I would find it"?

What actually happened, and was the fear justified?

→ On the publicly support, privately critique principle: Identify one current situation where you are publicly endorsing something you have genuine private concerns about.

Is there a legitimate private forum where those concerns can actually be heard, or have you been staying quiet because no such forum exists?

If the forum exists but you haven't used it: What is the specific conversation you have been avoiding, and when will you have it?

If no real forum exists: Is this a situation that calls for staying and advocating harder for one, or one that calls for stepping away?

→ Authenticity is not about saying everything you think everywhere. It is about ensuring that what you say publicly and what you believe privately are not permanently disconnected.

The Home-Building Metaphor

Let me share a metaphor that changed how I approach authenticity and relationships: the home-building metaphor.

For most of my adult life, I built my emotional home in other people and external things. I built my home in my leaders, in my profession as a pilot, and in the belief systems and organizational structures that governed my actions. I built my home in people I considered friends, in roles that gave me identity and influence, and in achievements and recognition.

But when you build your home in other people, you give them the power to make you homeless.

When your emotional security relies on external factors like approval, positions, achievements, and relationships, your sense of well-being becomes dependent on conditions you cannot control.

For years, I lived off the scraps of others' acceptance, validation, and inclusion, thinking of that as my home. My sense of feeling "at home" was dictated by how much they welcomed me into theirs, rather than how at home I felt within myself.

The defining moment came during a meeting with my wing commander. When he remarked that I owed my position to him, the expected response was gratitude and deference.

Instead, something deep within me jumped out and pushed back against that social conditioning: "No, sir, that is not true. I just would not be working in an organization led by you." I said.

The silence that followed was excruciating. I felt simultaneously brilliant and terrified. I didn't know whether to backtrack and explain or to sit in the discomfort. But I knew I had to remain quiet.

That moment marked my first step toward reclaiming my authenticity. It was also the beginning of my understanding that my home belongs nowhere outside of myself and is not validated by any external source. I am the architect, the builder, and the designer of my own sense of being at home in the world.

The Permission Paradox

One of the most crucial insights about authenticity is that the permission we often seek can only come from ourselves.

Most of us are unconsciously waiting for permission to be who we really are. Permission from our parents, employers, industry, communities, or peers. We are waiting for someone to tell us it's okay to care about what genuinely interests us, to pursue our real passions, and to express our authentic values and perspectives.

But no one else can grant you that permission because no one else truly knows who you are. They only know the versions of you they have encountered, which may be quite limited if you have been performing personas rather than expressing authenticity.

This challenge is particularly difficult for high achievers who have been rewarded for adaptability and meeting external expectations. The very skills that contributed to their success, reading what systems want and delivering on those expectations, can hinder authentic expression.

I had to give myself permission to be interested in things that weren't traditionally valued in a military context. I had to give myself permission to value outcomes that couldn't be measured by rank or awards. I had to give myself permission to care about individual development, organizational health, and business strategy in ways that transcended institutional requirements.

This doesn't mean rejecting everything about your previous identity or context. It means consciously deciding which aspects to keep based on what authentically represents you, rather than what serves external systems.

ACTION STEP: Build Your Home Inside Yourself

→ Map where you have been building your emotional home. In each of the areas below, write what you have been depending on externally for your sense of security, worth, or identity:

Professional: Which title, role, organization, or recognition have you been building your home in?

Relational: Whose approval, inclusion, or validation have you been treating as a requirement for feeling at home?

Achievement: Which accomplishments, credentials, or outcomes have you tied to your sense of fundamental worth?

→ On the permission paradox: Name one thing you have been waiting for permission to pursue, express, or become. Then write down who you have been waiting for permission from, and why that person or institution is the one you chose.

→ Now write one sentence granting yourself that permission. "I give myself permission to ________."

→ You are the architect of your home. What is one structural change that would make that home more genuinely yours?

The Courage Requirement

Authenticity requires courage because it involves vulnerability. When you stop performing and start to be real, you risk facing rejection, criticism, or simply not being understood.

What if the real you isn't as impressive as the persona you've maintained? What if people don't appreciate your authentic interests, values, or perspectives as much as they liked the version of you that was trying to please them?

These fears are often based on real experiences. Perhaps you faced criticism or rejection when you showed your authentic self in earlier contexts. Maybe you learned that certain parts of yourself weren't acceptable in your family, school, or work environment.

But the fear of not being authentic ultimately outweighs the fear of being rejected for being authentic.

When you are performing, constantly anxious about being discovered, you find yourself managing impressions, monitoring reactions, and adjusting your expressions in an attempt to maintain approval. This process is exhausting. While being authentic may lead to occasional rejection, it liberates you from the constant effort of maintaining a false identity. In being true to yourself, you attract people and opportunities that genuinely align with who you are, rather than who you think you should be.

The Integration Challenge

True authenticity is not about expressing every thought and feeling without a filter. Instead, it involves integrating all aspects of who you are into a coherent way of being that is honest, effective, and sustainable. This means bringing together your values, capabilities, interests, and personality in ways that advance your personal development and enable you to contribute value to others.

For me, authenticity meant integrating the strategic thinking I developed in military planning with the individual development focus that had always interested me personally. It involved merging the systems optimization skills I acquired in aviation with my curiosity about business strategy, which had remained dormant throughout my military career. Rather than viewing these as separate or potentially conflicting aspects of myself, I learned to see them as different facets of the same core identity: someone who helps leaders and organizations operate more effectively during periods of pressure and transition. Authenticity, I discovered, is not a new self you construct. It is an existing self finally given room to operate.

The Level 5 Leadership Connection

In his book Good to Great, Jim Collins identifies what he calls "Level 5 Leadership" as the type of leadership that characterizes truly exceptional organizations.

Level 5 leaders exhibit a paradoxical blend of intense professional will and personal humility. They are ambitious for their organizations while remaining modest about their personal contributions. They are fierce about achieving results, yet gentle in their personal interactions.

Collins discovered that the most charismatic, celebrity-like leaders, whom he calls Level 4 leaders, often achieve short-term success but rarely build lasting greatness. Their focus on personal image and dramatic leadership styles ultimately limits their long-term effectiveness. In contrast, Level 5 leaders are often described as quiet, understated, or even awkward in their demeanor, but they consistently produce superior results because they prioritize what actually works over what appears impressive.

This research aligns with what I have learned about authenticity. Trying to appear as a leader often prevents you from being an effective leader. When you stop worrying about how you are perceived and start focusing on creating value, your natural leadership abilities can emerge.

ACTION STEP: Integrate Your Identity

→ On the courage requirement: Identify the specific cost you have been paying for performing rather than being authentic. Not the abstract cost but the concrete, daily one.

How much energy do you spend each week managing impressions, monitoring reactions, or maintaining a persona that isn't fully yours?

What opportunities, relationships, or expressions have you declined because the real version of you didn't feel acceptable in that context?

→ On integration: Draw two columns. In the left column, list the capabilities, experiences, and values you developed in your previous context—the ones that feel most distinctly yours, even if they don't fit neatly into your current setting.

In the right column, write the capabilities, curiosities, and values that feel authentic to who you are now—the ones you have been keeping separate or compartmentalizing.

→ Look for the thread that connects both columns. That thread is your integrated identity, the core of what you uniquely offer. Write it in one sentence: "I am someone who ________, applied to ________."

→ On Level 5 Leadership: Identify one area where you have been optimizing for appearing effective rather than being effective. What would you do differently this week if you cared only about the result and not at all about how the result made you look?

The Empathy and Compassion Distinction

Authentic leadership involves recognizing the difference between empathy and compassion, between feeling someone else's pain and taking action to help alleviate it.

Empathy involves sharing in the feelings of others. For example, if you see someone being crushed by a boulder, empathy would mean feeling that same crushing sensation, which can render you helpless to help.

Compassion, on the other hand, means recognizing that someone is suffering and doing everything within your power to assist them. Compassion is empathy plus action.

As leaders, we need compassion more than empathy. We must genuinely care about our team's successes while also challenging them directly about their performance. Author Kim Scott calls this "radical candor," the intersection of caring personally and challenging directly.

Excessive empathy without challenge can lead to what Scott calls "ruinous empathy," where difficult conversations are avoided for fear of hurting feelings, even if those conversations are crucial for their development. Conversely, too much challenge without care can result in "obnoxious aggression," where demands are made without investing in relationships. Neither caring nor challenging leads to "manipulative insincerity," where there is neither support nor honesty. Authentic leadership requires a balance of caring and challenging, as both elements are essential for helping individuals reach their potential.

The Service Integration

As we conclude this chapter, it's important to connect authenticity to service, because authentic expression is ultimately about contributing your unique gifts to a cause greater than yourself.

The reason authenticity matters is that the world needs what you can uniquely offer. Your distinct combination of experience, perspective, skills, and values can address challenges and serve others in ways that no one else can.

However, you cannot share your unique gifts if you are busy trying to be someone else. You can't serve authentically if you are performing personas that disconnect you from your true capabilities.

When I stopped trying to conform to the role of a traditional business consultant and embraced my identity as someone with military operational experience addressing civilian leadership challenges, I was finally able to serve clients in genuinely distinctive ways.

When you stop trying to fit into established categories and start expressing your authentic nature, you not only feel better, but you also become more valuable to the people you are meant to serve.

Authenticity, fully expressed, stops being about you. When you are no longer spending energy maintaining a false version of yourself, you gain the capacity to see others clearly, meet genuine needs, and offer what the world actually requires. That is where this journey has been heading all along.

REFLECTION: Lead with Compassion and Close the Chapter

→ On the empathy and compassion distinction: Think of a person on your team or in your life right now who needs a difficult conversation, one you have been avoiding out of care for their feelings.

Are you practicing compassion and caring personally, while challenging directly? Or ruinous empathy, caring so much about their comfort that you are withholding something they actually need?

What is the one specific thing you would say if you combined genuine care with genuine directness, and when will you say it?

→ On service integration: Complete this sentence in writing: "The unique combination of experience, perspective, and capability that only I can bring to the people I serve is ________."

If you struggled to complete it, that difficulty is itself important information. It means the authenticity work is still in progress, which is not a failure. It is an invitation to keep going.

→ Closing synthesis: Look back at all eight chapters of this journey and name one specific way you are different today than when you began. Not what you know differently. Who you are differently.

→ That difference is the foundation from which you will serve. The next chapter is not about learning something new. It is about expressing what you have already become.

CHAPTER 9

Service—The Ultimate Expression

The email arrived on a Friday afternoon, three months after I had completed a major operational improvement project for a mid-sized manufacturing company.

The CEO was writing to inform me that the changes we had implemented were not only improving their bottom line but also transforming the work experience for their 200 employees.

He wrote: "I wanted to let you know that yesterday, for the first time in fifteen years, I walked through our production floor and heard people laughing, not just once or twice, but throughout the day. The efficiency improvements eliminated the constant crisis mode that had kept everyone stressed and overwhelmed. People now have time to think, collaborate, and actually enjoy their work again. You didn't just help us optimize our processes; you helped us remember why we started this company in the first place."

I read that email three times before the full impact hit me. This was what true service looked like: not merely delivering technical results or fulfilling contractual obligations, but using my authentic capabilities to help individuals and organizations realize their potential.

In that moment, I understood something that would reshape my thoughts about work, success, and life purpose. True service occurs when your authentic gifts meet genuine needs in ways that create far greater value than you originally intended. Service is not something you do in addition to your work; rather, it becomes your work when you align your authentic capabilities with opportunities to contribute to something larger than yourself.

The Walt and Roy Dynamic in Service

Throughout this book, we have discussed the importance of integrating vision with execution and dreams with practical implementation. In service, this integration becomes crucial because good intentions without effective execution do not actually benefit anyone.

Every Walt Disney needs a Roy Disney; every visionary needs a planner. Every idea needs someone who can turn it into reality.

In the realm of service, you need both the inspiration to envision what is possible and the capability to make it happen. You need the compassion to care about outcomes and the competence to create them.

I've seen many people with generous hearts but insufficient skills trying to serve others, often leading to disappointing results for everyone involved. Conversely, I've encountered individuals with impressive abilities who lack genuine care for the people they are supposed to be helping, and those relationships rarely create lasting value.

True service requires both care and competence. You must genuinely want to help, and you have to actually be able to help. This is why the work we've done in previous chapters—developing awareness, overcoming resistance, clarifying identity, facing fears, letting go of limitations, authentically redefining yourself and taking aligned action—is essential preparation for meaningful service.

You cannot give what you do not possess. You cannot help others navigate transitions you have not learned to navigate yourself. You cannot serve from a place of authenticity if you have not done the work of discovering and expressing who you truly are.

REFLECTION: Define What True Service Looks Like for You

→ Think about a moment in your work or life when you knew—not just thought, but knew—that you had genuinely served someone. Not a transaction. Not a deliverable. A moment when your authentic capability met a real need and created something that surprised even you.

What were you doing? What capability were you drawing on?

What did the person or organization you served actually receive beyond what was originally asked for?

How did it feel different from the work you do that is merely competent or merely well-intentioned?

→ Now apply the Walt and Roy test to your current work. On a blank page, draw two columns:

Walt: The vision, compassion, and authentic care you bring to what you do.

Roy: The competence, execution capability, and practical skill to make it real.

→ Which column is stronger right now? Is there one specific investment you could make this month to strengthen it?

From Crisis to Clarity: When Military Frameworks Meet Business Transformation

The principles I've shared throughout this book aren't just theoretical concepts but the foundation of how I serve clients today. In the years since that terrifying parking lot moment, I've discovered that the combination of military crisis leadership, operational excellence methodologies, and authentic transformation creates something powerful: the ability to help executives navigate uncertainty while driving measurable results.

This integration of crisis decision-making frameworks with business transformation isn't accidental. When you've spent nearly three decades making decisions at 30,000 feet, where mistakes can be catastrophic, you develop a particular approach to clarity under pressure. When you combine that with Lean Six Sigma operational excellence and the vulnerability work we've explored in this book, something unique emerges.

I work with C-suite executives and business owners who face their own versions of "caterpillar soup" moments, times when everything familiar is dissolving, and they need both the strategic clarity to navigate uncertainty and the operational frameworks to drive measurable results. Whether they're preparing for an exit, integrating post-acquisition, or leading through a crisis, the work requires both transformation and execution.

The authenticity principles we've explored aren't separate from operational excellence. They're what make operational excellence sustainable. You can't lead a transformation from a place of performance. You can't create lasting organizational change without addressing the identity and resistance patterns that created the original problems.

This is why my approach combines executive coaching with operational consulting and M&A advisory work. Real transformation requires all three:

the internal work of authentic leadership development, the external work of system and process optimization, and the strategic work of building enterprise value.

If you are curious about how these frameworks might apply to your specific situation, whether you are navigating a leadership transition, preparing for an exit, or working to optimize operations while developing your executive team, you can learn more about my work at www.benmorley.com. The integration of authentic transformation with measurable business results creates possibilities that traditional approaches can't achieve.

The Resourcefulness Over Resources Principle

One of the most powerful principles for effective service is prioritizing resourcefulness over resources. Great service rarely demands perfect resources, but instead, it requires creative, committed individuals who can accomplish much with limited means.

I recall a humanitarian mission we supported that taught me this lesson profoundly. We were tasked with delivering medical supplies and food to remote islands in the South Pacific that had not been visited by U.S. military aircraft since World War II.

The challenge was that these airfields were not suitable for our C-17 aircraft. Although the runways could bear our weight, the taxiways could not, meaning we could not taxi off the runway to unload. The solution demanded resourcefulness rather than additional resources.

We coordinated with local authorities to temporarily shut down the airfield while we unloaded the aircraft directly on the runway. To minimize the risk of mechanical issues during this vulnerable time, we kept the engines running throughout the entire unloading process. It wasn't the standard approach, but it was how we could serve the people who needed what we were carrying.

Meaningful service often necessitates this type of creative problem-solving. You use whatever you have at your disposal in any way necessary to meet genuine needs.

In my consulting work, I regularly witness this principle in action. The clients who create the most value for their customers are not necessarily the ones with the largest budgets or the most sophisticated systems. They are the ones with teams committed to finding solutions, regardless of resource constraints.

One of my clients, a small manufacturing company competing against much larger competitors, built a reputation for customizing solutions to meet unique customer requirements. While they lacked the resources to compete on price or scale, they demonstrated resourcefulness in solving problems that larger competitors could not or would not address. Their willingness to figure out how to serve customers with complex needs, often requiring creative approaches, ultimately made them so valuable that they were acquired by one of those larger competitors seeking access to their problem-solving capabilities.

The Value Over Effort Distinction

In service, as in all areas of life, it's crucial to reward value creation rather than effort expenditure.

I often observe people confusing busyness with productivity, working hard with working effectively, and hours spent with results achieved. Many measure their service by the effort they put in rather than by the value they create. However, the people you serve do not care about how hard you are working. They care about whether you are solving their problems.

They do not want to hear about your struggles. They want to see your solutions. While effort does matter, it is not sufficient on its own. Sometimes, the most valuable service requires very little effort because it stems from deep expertise and authentic capability.

I learned this lesson from observing master craftsmen in various fields. For example, a skilled surgeon can solve a complex problem in thirty minutes that would require someone less experienced hours to address, and the results are far better. An experienced pilot can handle emergency situations with calm efficiency, potentially saving lives, while a less skilled individual might panic, making the situation worse.

The value lies not in the time invested but in the capability applied.

In my consulting work, I've noticed that my most valuable contributions often feel effortless to me because they are natural applications of capabilities I have spent decades developing. What feels like a simple observation to me can be a breakthrough insight for a client, as it comes from a perspective they do not have access to. The goal is not to make service feel difficult to demonstrate its value. Instead, it's to develop capabilities that enable you to create significant value efficiently and sustainably.

ACTION STEP: Apply Resourcefulness Over Resources

→ On resourcefulness: Identify a situation in your current work where you have been waiting for better resources—more time, more budget, more staff, more access—before you can serve at the level you want to. Name it specifically.

Now ask: What is the minimum viable version of this service that I could deliver with exactly what I have today?

What would a C-17 crew on a South Pacific runway do with this constraint—keep the engines running and unload anyway?

→ On value over effort: Think about the work you do that creates the most genuine value for the people you serve. Is that work typically your most effortful work, or is it the work that comes most naturally from deep capability?

If your highest-value contributions feel relatively effortless, are you charging and positioning for the value created—or apologizing for how quickly it came?

If your highest-effort work isn't creating the highest value, what does that signal about where your genuine capability actually lives?

→ Name one shift in how you price, position, or direct your energy that would better align your effort with your actual value creation.

The Empathy and Compassion Integration

Earlier in the book, I mentioned the difference between empathy and compassion, which becomes critically important in service. Empathy means feeling what others feel, while compassion involves recognizing others' suffering and taking action to alleviate it.

Empathy without action can be counterproductive in service contexts. If you feel overwhelmed by someone else's pain, it can render you less capable of helping them. By taking on their emotional state, you lose the clarity and objectivity needed to identify solutions.

Compassion, on the other hand, allows you to care deeply while maintaining the emotional equilibrium necessary for effective action. I learned this lesson during my years of training pilots. When a student struggled, feeling empathy would have meant sharing their frustration, anxiety, and self-doubt. This would have made me less effective as an instructor. Compassion meant recognizing their struggle, understanding what it felt like to be in their position, and using that understanding to provide the guidance and support they needed to improve.

Sometimes, compassion involves challenging someone to do better than they think they can. Other times, it looks like offering encouragement when they are ready to give up or setting boundaries when they expect you to solve problems they need to tackle themselves. The key is to maintain care for their well-being while focusing on what genuinely helps them progress toward their goals.

REFLECTION: Practice Compassion in Your Current Service

→ Identify one person you are currently serving with whom you have been practicing empathy when compassion was called for.

Are you absorbing their emotional state in a way that is reducing your effectiveness, your clarity, or your willingness to give them the honest challenge they actually need?

What is the specific conversation, feedback, or boundary you have been avoiding because empathy made it feel too painful to deliver?

→ Now consider: What does compassion (care plus action) look like in this situation? There are three forms:

Challenge: Asking more of them than they are currently asking of themselves.

Encouragement: Offering genuine belief in their capacity when they are ready to quit.

Boundary: Declining to solve what they need to solve themselves.

→ Which of these three does this person actually need from you right now? Commit to delivering it not from emotional distance, but from the grounded care of someone who genuinely wants them to grow.

The Long-Term Perspective

True service operates from a long-term perspective rather than seeking immediate gratification or quick fixes. This becomes especially important when helping people through transitions, as transformation takes time. The most meaningful changes often happen gradually, with periods of apparent stagnation followed by sudden breakthroughs.

In my work with business owners preparing for M&A, the operational improvements we implement often take months to show measurable results. However, when they do appear, the impact is often dramatic, not only on company valuation but also on organizational capability and employee satisfaction.

There is always the temptation to seek faster approaches, immediate wins, or dramatic interventions that deliver quick results. Yet, sustainable service requires patience with natural timing and trust in gradual processes. This long-term perspective also means measuring success differently. Instead of focusing solely on immediate outcomes, you focus on capability development, system improvements, and foundational changes that will create ongoing value long after your direct involvement ends.

The best service makes itself unnecessary over time. You are not trying to create dependence but rather to build independence. You are not solving problems for people; you are helping them develop the capability to solve problems themselves.

The Multiplication Effect

One of the most rewarding aspects of authentic service is called the "multiplication effect." When you help someone become more effective, they can use that increased effectiveness to help others. When you improve an organization's operations, those improvements benefit everyone who interacts with that organization.

The best service creates expanding circles of positive impact that extend far beyond your direct involvement. For instance, the manufacturing company I mentioned earlier didn't just benefit from the operational improvements we implemented. Their enhanced efficiency allowed them to offer better service to their customers, create improved working conditions for their employees, and generate better returns for their investors. Because of this, their customers could better serve their own customers, and so on.

This multiplication effect illustrates why it is essential to focus on fundamental improvements rather than superficial fixes. When you help someone develop genuine capability, that capability becomes a permanent asset that they can apply to multiple situations over time. Similarly, when you assist an organization in building better systems, those systems continue creating value long after your involvement. When you help a leader develop authentic confidence and clear decision-making frameworks, they can utilize those capabilities to navigate challenges you never anticipated.

ACTION STEP: Design for the Long Term and the Multiplication Effect

→ On the long-term perspective: Identify one area of your current service where you have been optimizing for immediate results at the cost of lasting impact.

What would the long-term version of your service look like in this situation? What capability would the person or organization have built that they currently still depend on you to provide?

What is one thing you could do differently starting now to move from solving their problem to building their ability to solve it?

→ On the multiplication effect: Map one circle of expanding impact from your work. Start with the person or organization you most directly serve, then trace outward:

Who do they serve, and how does your work change what they can offer those people?

Who do those people serve, and what becomes possible for them as a result?

→ Most people who serve well dramatically underestimate the reach of their impact because they only measure what they can directly observe. Write out two or three rings of your multiplication circle. The picture that emerges is not hypothetical. It is already happening.

The Authenticity Requirement

We cannot discuss service without considering authenticity, because inauthentic service is not really service at all.

True service can only stem from your authentic nature. You cannot sustainably serve in ways that contradict who you really are. You cannot help others find their authentic path if you are not walking your own.

This is why all the work we have done in previous chapters is essential preparation for meaningful service. You must know who you are before you can offer who you are. You need to be clear about your own values before you can assist others in clarifying theirs. You need to have worked through your own resistance and fears before you can help others navigate theirs.

Authentic service feels natural rather than forced. It energizes you rather than draining you, and aligns with your capabilities rather than requiring you to be someone you are not.

When I work with clients on operational improvements, it does not feel like work because it is a natural expression of how my mind functions. When I coach executives through challenging decisions, it feels meaningful because it draws on experiences I have genuinely had, rather than on theories I have merely learned. This does not imply that service is always easy or comfortable. Sometimes, authentic service requires you to stretch beyond your current comfort zone, but it should never demand that you violate your core nature or fundamental values.

The Integration Challenge

As we conclude this book, I want to address the integration challenge: how to bring together all the elements we have explored into a coherent approach to living and working.

Awareness, resistance, identity, fear, letting go, redefinition, forward motion, authenticity, and service are not separate concepts to be mastered one at a time. They are interconnected aspects of human development that you will work with simultaneously throughout your life.

You do not finish the work of identity before moving on to authenticity. You do not resolve all resistance, only to never encounter it again. You do not achieve perfect awareness and then coast on that accomplishment.

These are ongoing practices that deepen and evolve as you grow, as circumstances change, and as you face new challenges. The goal is integration—developing the ability to work with these elements to become who you were meant to be and to contribute what you are meant to contribute.

The Continuous Evolution

Service, like everything else we've discussed, evolves over time. The ways you serve in your thirties will differ from how you serve in your fifties, not because your core nature changes, but because your capabilities, experiences, and circumstances continue to develop. The key is to remain open to how your service wants to evolve rather than getting locked into outdated definitions of what service looks like for you.

When I left the military, I thought I was giving up service for personal pursuits. What I discovered was that I was transitioning from one form of service to another, from serving national defense to serving individual and organizational development. The impulse to serve was always present; only the expression changed.

As you continue to grow, as your skills develop, as your understanding deepens, and as your life circumstances evolve, your service will continue to evolve, too. The question is not what form that service should take, but whether you are staying open to discovering what wants to emerge.

The Ultimate Integration

In the end, this entire book has been about one fundamental transformation: moving from living reactively to living authentically, from being shaped by external forces to consciously shaping your own direction, and from seeking approval to creating value. It's about discovering who you truly are underneath all the conditioning, expectations, and limiting beliefs, and then having the courage to express that authentic self in service of something meaningful.

The work is never finished because growth is never finished. But the foundation, once established, becomes the platform from which all future development occurs.

You do not need to have everything figured out to begin this work. You just need to be willing to start, to pay attention, to question assumptions, to face discomfort, to let go of what no longer serves you, and to take action aligned with who you are becoming rather than being limited by who you have been.

The world needs what you specifically have to offer. Your unique blend of experiences, perspectives, values, and skills enables you to solve problems and serve others in ways that no one else can.

However, you cannot share your unique gifts if you don't recognize them. You can't serve authentically if you are preoccupied with trying to be someone else. You won't create lasting value if your focus is on obtaining short-term approval rather than long-term contribution.

The journey from who you have been to who you are meant to be is not always comfortable, but it is always worthwhile. On the other side of that journey lies a life filled with meaning, impact, and genuine fulfillment that no external achievement can provide.

This is the ultimate service: becoming your true self so you can share your unique gifts with a world that desperately needs them.

The real question is not whether you are capable of this transformation, because you are. The question is whether you are willing to begin.

REFLECTION: The Ultimate Integration: Your Closing Synthesis

→ This is the final reflection of the book. It is not a checklist. It is an invitation to take stock of the entire journey before you turn toward what comes next.

Look back across all nine chapters. For each theme below, write one honest sentence about where you are—not where you wish you were, and not where you started. Where you actually are now:

Awareness: What am I now able to see about myself that I could not see before?

Resistance: What do I now recognize as the specific form my resistance most often takes?

Identity: What is the most honest description of who I actually am, separate from the roles I have played?

Fear: What fear have I faced, or begun to face, that I was avoiding when I started reading?

Letting Go: What have I released, or begun releasing, that was holding me in place?

Redefinition: What is the most authentic version of myself I am currently stepping into?

Forward Motion: What is the one aligned action I have taken, or committed to, that I would not have taken before?

Authenticity: In what specific way am I showing up more genuinely than I was?

Service: What unique gift am I now more prepared to offer, and to whom?

→ Now answer the book's final question—not rhetorically, but in writing, as a commitment:

"The one thing I am willing to begin—that I was not willing to begin before—is ________."

That is what service ultimately reveals: that the transformation was never only for you. Every mile of the cocoon, every sleepless night in the dissolution, and every moment of reaching in the dark was preparation not just for your sake, but for the people waiting on the other side of your becoming.

The butterfly doesn't fly alone. It carries what survived the soup into a world that needed it all along.

In the pages that follow, we return to where this journey began, and you will see, as I eventually did, just how far the flight has already taken you.

CONCLUSION

The View From Here

Back to the Parking Lot

Remember that parking lot? The one where I sat in my car, hands sweating, listening to my inner voice tell me I was about to be exposed as a fraud in my first civilian business meeting? At the time of writing this book, I drove past that parking lot. The building looks the same. The parking spaces are arranged exactly as they were five years ago. But everything else is different. I am different.

The meeting I was so terrified of led to a client relationship that transformed both their business and my understanding of what I was capable of contributing. The imposter syndrome that had me paralyzed eventually became a teacher, guiding me to distinguish between performing confidence and genuinely being confident in who I am. The voice that told me I didn't belong still resonates with me occasionally. But now I recognize it as resistance, trying to protect me from vulnerability by keeping me small. I've learned to thank it for caring about my safety while choosing to act and move forward anyway.

Five years ago, I could never have imagined writing this book. Not because I lacked the writing skills or stories to share, but because I didn't understand that my unconventional path from military aviation to business consulting was not a limitation to overcome. Instead, it was the unique combination of experiences that enabled me to serve my clients in ways that traditional consultants could not.

I didn't need to become someone else; I needed to become more fully myself. That is the journey I have attempted to map in these pages. And now, as we close, I want to return one final time to the image that has guided us throughout: the caterpillar, the cocoon, and the butterfly.

The Butterfly Looks Back

The butterfly, once fully emerged and dry-winged, cannot return to the cocoon. It cannot un-become what it has become. It cannot go back to crawling when it is capable of flight.

But the butterfly carries the caterpillar within it. Not as a limitation. Not as an identity. But as a foundation. The caterpillar's determination to consume, to grow, and to press against every constraint it encountered became the raw material for flight. Nothing essential was wasted. Everything was transformed.

When I drove past that parking lot last week, I wasn't dismissing the person who sat there five years ago, paralyzed by imposter syndrome and convinced he didn't belong. I was honoring him. He had the courage to enter the cocoon. He didn't know what would emerge, but he entered anyway. Without him, there is no me.

This is what I want you to understand about the transformation you are navigating: nothing essential will be lost. The capabilities, insights, values, and hard-won wisdom you have accumulated across every phase of your life are your imaginal cells. They are the building blocks that will survive the dissolution and reorganize into something capable of flight.

What is dissolved in the cocoon is not you. It is who you were required to be in a context that no longer fits.

The butterfly does not mourn the caterpillar. It flies.

What I Have Learned

If I could sit down with you over coffee and share the most important lessons from my journey, I would tell you that your unconventional path is your competitive advantage. Whatever makes your background different from others in your field is not a deficit to overcome but the source of the unique value you can create. Stop trying to fit into existing categories and start creating new ones that honor all of who you are.

Transformation requires dissolution. You cannot become a butterfly while remaining a caterpillar. At some point, everything familiar must dissolve into something that looks like soup before it can reorganize into something capable of flight. The discomfort you feel is evidence that real transformation is happening.

The cocoon is not a crisis. It is a process. The disorientation, isolation, and uncertainty you experience in transition are not symptoms of something going wrong. They are characteristics of something going right. Recognizing the cocoon for what it is changes everything about how you endure it.

Resistance often gets louder right before breakthroughs. When you are on the verge of significant growth, your internal resistance will do everything it can to keep you in your comfort zone. Learn to recognize this pattern. The intensity of the resistance is often proportional to the importance of what is trying to emerge.

Major transitions can feel like you are discarding decades of development and starting from zero. However, nothing essential is ever lost. The imaginal cells survive. Every capability you have developed, every lesson you have learned, and every relationship you have built all come with you in the next chapter, expressed in new forms.

Confidence comes from action, not the other way around. The butterfly doesn't wait until it feels confident before trying its wings. It tries its wings, and confidence follows. You will never feel completely ready for your next level of challenge. Act anyway.

Service is the highest expression of transformation. All the internal work is in service of becoming someone capable of contributing value that only you can provide.

The butterfly does not fly for its own sake. It pollinates. That is authentic service.

The view from here is worth every step of the climb. Transformation is hard work. There were times in my journey when I questioned whether the discomfort, uncertainty, and vulnerability were truly worth it. Looking back now, I can say with absolute certainty that every uncomfortable moment was worthwhile for the life and work that emerged on the other side.

How These Principles Transform Business Results

The frameworks in this book form the foundation of my work with executives and organizations today. Integrating authentic transformation with operational excellence has led to documented results that traditional approaches could not achieve:

- $13.5 million in revenue increases across Fortune 500 engagements, because when leaders operate from a place of authenticity rather than simply focusing on performance, they make fundamentally different strategic decisions.

- Eighty-four percent efficiency gains through operational optimization, because the resistance and identity work we have explored in this book directly impacts how organizations implement change.

- Successful exit strategy preparation for companies with an enterprise value ranging from $5 million to $30 million, because the same principles that guide personal transformations also facilitate organizational transformations.

- Post-acquisition integration success for private equity firms and strategic acquirers, because the principles of navigating identity dissolution and emergence pertain to the cultural integration challenges that can determine M&A success or failure.

This is not a coincidence. Organizations, like individuals, go through cocoon phases. The companies that emerge stronger from major transitions are the ones that understand the dissolution as a feature, not a bug.

Working Together: What Is Possible

If you are a C-suite executive, business owner, or organizational leader who recognizes yourself in these pages, you might be curious what it would look like to apply these frameworks to your specific situation. The work takes different forms depending on what you're navigating.

- **Executive coaching** that integrates authentic leadership development with crisis decision-making frameworks. Unlike traditional coaching that emphasizes only behavioral change, this work focuses on transforming identity, resistance, and fear patterns that limit strategic clarity while simultaneously building the systemic decision-making capabilities that yield breakthrough results.

- **Operational excellence consulting** that applies Lean Six Sigma methodologies through the lens of organizational transformation. By combining organizational optimization with the principles of awareness and letting go that we've discussed, organizations can cultivate the capability to continuously improve and adapt.

- **M&A advisory services** that prepare companies for successful exits by enhancing both enterprise value and organizational capability. The same transformation principles that support individual growth also guide the systematic preparation for major business transitions.

- **Post-acquisition integration support** for private equity firms and strategic acquirers who need both strategic frameworks and cultural integration expertise to realize projected synergies.

- **Professional speaking** engagements that translate crisis leadership and operational excellence into practical frameworks your teams can immediately apply.

You can discover how these frameworks might apply to your specific situation at www.benmorley.com.

Closing this book is just the beginning. The real work begins with the decisions you make tomorrow morning, the conversations you have next week, and the choices you face next month when resistance shows up and tries to convince you to abandon the growth that is calling you.

Your transformation serves more than just you. When you put in the hard work to become the person you're meant to be, you become capable of contributing value that wasn't possible when you operated from a limited version of yourself. The butterfly serves the entire ecosystem. Your transformation ripples out to benefit everyone you serve.

The Journey Continues

At the beginning of this book, I invited you to stop living reactively and start living authentically. To stop trying to fit into someone else's definition of success and start creating your own based on who you truly are and what you genuinely can contribute.

That invitation remains open.

The caterpillar doesn't need to understand the butterfly in order to become one. It simply needs to stop resisting the process that is already underway.

So I will ask you again: Are you ready to enter your cocoon?

Not to have everything figured out. Not to eliminate all uncertainty. Not to feel completely confident and ready to start. Just to take the next step. To trust that what needs to dissolve will dissolve. To trust that what is essential will survive. And to trust that what assembles on the other side of the soup will exceed anything the caterpillar could have imagined.

It is time to trust the cocoon.

THANK YOU FOR READING!

To support you on the journey ahead, I've put together an additional resource—it's yours as my gift, completely free.

Scan the QR Code:

I appreciate your interest in my book and value your feedback, as it helps me improve future versions. I would appreciate it if you could leave your invaluable review on Amazon.com with your feedback. Thank you!

www.ingramcontent.com/pod-product-compliance
Lightning Source LLC
LaVergne TN
LVHW100528110826
845146LV00002B/812

* 9 7 9 8 9 0 1 5 8 2 0 7 7 *